SO-AHJ-668

Buy 4/...

Created 2000
last thru 2004
Use 6

THE LAW OF
CAPITAL PUNISHMENT

by
Margaret C. Jasper, Esq.

Oceana's Legal Almanac Series:
Law for the Layperson

1998
Oceana Publications, Inc.
Dobbs Ferry, N.Y.

You may order this or any other Oceana publications by visiting Oceana's Web Site at http://www.oceanalaw.com

Library of Congress Cataloging-in-Publication Data

JAN 6 2000

Jasper, Margaret C.
    The law of capital punishment / by Margaret C. Jasper.
        p.   cm.— (Oceana's legal almanac series. Law for the layperson)
    Includes bibliographical references.
    ISBN 0-379-11331-7 (alk. paper)
    1. Capital punishment—United States. I. Title. II. Series.
KF9227.C2J37   1998   98-7740
345.73'0773—dc21   CIP

Oceana's Legal Almanac Series: Law for the Layperson
ISSN: 1075-7376

©1998 by Oceana Publications, Inc.

Manufactured in the United States of America on acid-free paper.

To My Husband Chris

**Your love and support
are my motivation and inspiration**

-and-

In memory of my son, Jimmy

ABOUT THE AUTHOR

MARGARET C. JASPER is an attorney engaged in the general practice of law in South Salem, New York, concentrating in the areas of personal injury and entertainment law. Ms. Jasper holds a Juris Doctor degree from Pace University School of Law, White Plains, New York, is a member of the New York and Connecticut bars, and is certified to practice before the United States District Courts for the Southern and Eastern Districts of New York, and the United States Supreme Court. Ms. Jasper has been appointed to the panel of arbitrators of the American Arbitration Association and the law guardian panel for the Family Court of the State of New York, and is a New York State licensed real estate broker and member of the Westchester County Board of Realtors, operating as Jasper Real Estate, in South Salem, New York.

Ms. Jasper is the author and general editor of the following legal almanacs: Juvenile Justice and Children's Law; Marriage and Divorce; Estate Planning; The Law of Contracts; The Law of Dispute Resolution; Law for the Small Business Owner; The Law of Personal Injury; Real Estate Law for the Homeowner and Broker; Everyday Legal Forms; Dictionary of Selected Legal Terms; The Law of Medical Malpractice; The Law of Product Liability; The Law of No-Fault Insurance; The Law of Immigration; The Law of Libel and Slander; The Law of Buying and Selling; Elder Law; The Right to Die; AIDS Law; The Law of Obscenity and Pornography; The Law of Child Custody; The Law of Debt Collection; Consumer Rights Law; Bankruptcy Law for the Individual Debtor; Victim's Rights Law; Animal Rights Law; Workers' Compensation Law; Employee Rights in the Workplace; Probate Law; Environmental Law; Labor Law; and The Americans with Disabilities Act.

TABLE OF CONTENTS

INTRODUCTION

In the past twenty years, the reintroduction of capital punishment in the United States has steadily increased. Presently, all but twelve states and the District of Columbia have capital punishment statutes. In addition, the Federal government has recently expanded its application of the death penalty to a number of federal offenses.

Nevertheless, the general worldwide trend has been towards abolition of the death penalty, and more than 100 countries have done away with capital punishment either by law or by practice.

This almanac sets forth an overview of capital punishment in the United States, including the reasons which led to its abolition by the U.S. Supreme Court in 1972, and its subsequent reappearance in 1976. This almanac examines the statistical application of the death penalty according to characteristics such as age, gender, and race, and the methods by which executions are carried out among the states.

The arguments for and against capital punishment are also presented, including legal representation, deterrence, cost and the concern over unjustified executions of innocent individuals. Finally, this almanac discusses the international status of the death penalty among abolitionist and retentionist countries.

The Appendix provides applicable statutes, resource directories, and other pertinent information and data. The Glossary contains definitions of many of the terms used throughout the almanac.

CHAPTER 1:

AN OVERVIEW

In General

The death penalty has been utilized as a form of punishment in America since colonial times, and public execution of criminals was common during the 19th and early 20th centuries. One of the last public executions was conducted in 1936, when 20,000 people gathered to watch the hanging of a young Black male in Kentucky. By the early 1960's, most states had stopped enforcing the death penalty.

Ban on the Death Penalty in the United States

In 1972, the United States Supreme Court held that the death penalty was cruel and unusual punishment in violation of the Eighth and Fourteenth Amendments to the U.S. Constitution (*Georgia v. Furman*, 408 U.S. 238). Prior to *Furman*, the constitutionality of the death penalty was rarely challenged.

This landmark holding was based on a review of the existing capital punishment statutes. The Supreme Court did not find the practice itself to be unconstitutional, but rather the arbitrary and unpredictable manner in which the sentences were being imposed.

The Court concluded that the evidence proved the death penalty was being sought and/or handed down primarily in cases where the offender was poor, or a member of a minority group, and that death sentences were being imposed without any statutory guidelines or standards. As part of its decision, the Court reversed death sentences in many pending cases involving a variety of state statutes.

Reintroduction of the Death Penalty in the United States

In response to the *Furman* decision, a number of states rewrote their death penalty statutes in order to satisfy the scrutiny of the Court. In 1976, the Supreme Court lifted its ban on capital punishment, holding that its previous concerns with the unfair and arbitrary application of the death sentence had been addressed by the redrafted state statutes (*Gregg v. Georgia*, 428 U.S. 153).

Florida, Georgia, and Texas were among the first state statutes to survive the Supreme Court's scrutiny. The Court held that these statutes provided the necessary guidance to prevent the arbitrary application of the death penalty by trial juries.

The text of the Florida Death Penalty Statute is set forth in the Appendix.

Although the specific death penalty provisions of state statutes vary greatly, the typical statute now requires a bifurcated trial in capital cases, i.e. one which is divided into two components. During the first stage, the jury determines guilt or innocence.

If the defendant is judged innocent, the trial is over. If the defendant is found guilty, the trial proceeds to its second stage at which point the jury—or in some states, the judge—chooses imprisonment or death in light of any aggravating or mitigating circumstances.

Present Application of the Death Penalty

Death Penalty Jurisdictions

Since 1976, 38 states and the Federal government have enacted death penalty statutes patterned after those the Supreme Court upheld in *Gregg*. Twelve states and the District of Columbia have not yet authorized any type of death penalty statute.

A table of non-death penalty states is set forth in the Appendix.

Statistics

In 1996, 45 prisoners were executed in nineteen states. These prisoners had been on death row an average of 10 years and 5 months before being executed. Of the total, 36 of the executions were carried out by lethal injection; 7 by electrocution, 1 by hanging and 1 by firing squad. Arkansas alone executed 3 men in 3 hours by lethal injection. In addition, 3,219 prisoners were under sentence of death as of December 1996.

Tables setting forth the number of prisoners executed and the number of prisoners on death row in 1996, categorized by state, are set forth in the Appendix.

The 1996 figure of prisoners on death row is almost double the number of prisoners under sentence of death in 1986, and 25 times higher than the number of prisoners under sentence of death in 1953. A table setting forth the number of prisoners under sentence of death from 1953 through 1996 is also set forth in the Appendix.

According to the Bureau of Justice Statistics (BJS), in the first 11 months of 1997 alone, more than 70 prisoners were executed in 16 states—the highest total since the Supreme Court lifted the ban in 1976.

Of the 70 executions, Texas accounted for 36—exceeding the highest number of executions in one state in a single year since the federal government began an annual count in 1930.

A table setting forth the number of executions conducted from 1930 through 1997 is set forth in the Appendix.

Capital Offenses

Nearly all state capital punishment statutes differ with respect to which crimes constitute capital offenses. For example, some states—such as Delaware—limit the death penalty to first degree murder, while other states—such as Arkansas—may hand down a death sentence for a number of other crimes, such as treason.

A table of capital offenses categorized by state is set forth in the Appendix.

In addition, the Federal Government has statutorily authorized the death penalty for a number of offenses. A table of Federal death penalty offenses categorized by statute is set forth in the Appendix.

Methods of Execution

As set forth below, prisoners are executed in the United States by any one of five methods, which vary from state to state, including: (i) hanging; (ii) firing squad; (iii) electrocution; (iv) lethal gas; and (v) lethal injection.

Hanging

The traditional mode of execution—hanging—is still authorized in Delaware, New Hampshire and Washington. There are many drawbacks to this method of execution. For example, if the drop is too short, there will be a slow and agonizing death by strangulation. If the drop is too long, there is a risk of decapitation.

Firing Squad

The firing squad is still authorized in two states: Idaho and Utah. In carrying out this method of execution, the prisoner is generally strapped into a chair and a hood is placed over his or her head. A target is pinned to the prisoner's chest. There are usually a minimum of five marksmen. They are provided with loaded weapons except for one which is filled with blanks. None of the marksmen know which gun contains the blanks. On orders, they take aim at the target and fire.

Electrocution

Throughout the twentieth century, electrocution was the most widely employed method of execution in the United States. Electrocution is still authorized in eleven states.

In carrying out this method of execution, the prisoner is taken into the electrocution chamber and strapped into a chair. Electrodes are fastened to the prisoner's head and legs. A switch is tripped which sends high voltage throughout the prisoner's body. There has been much criticism over this method of execution, particularly after one prisoner's death was reportedly prolonged by as much as 14 minutes, during which he literally caught on fire (The 1983 execution of John Evans in Alabama).

Lethal Gas

The administration of lethal gas was an effort to improve on execution by electrocution. In carrying out this method of execution, the prisoner is also taken into a chamber and strapped into a chair. A container of sulfuric acid is placed underneath the chair. The chamber is sealed, and cyanide is dropped into the acid to form a lethal gas.

Unfortunately, there have also been reported mishaps during the administration of lethal gas. In one instance, it took almost 11 minutes for the prisoner to succumb to the lethal gas, during which time he suffered violent convulsions (The 1992 execution of Don Harding in Arizona).

In 1996, the Ninth Circuit Court of Appeals in California, where the gas chamber has been used since 1933, ruled that execution by lethal gas is a "cruel and unusual punishment," paving the way to abolition of this method of execution.

Lethal Injection

Execution by lethal injection is the most recently devised method of execution. In carrying out death by lethal injection, the prisoner is strapped down and a lethal mixture of drugs is administered intravenously.

Most view lethal injection as the most humane and acceptable manner of execution, although it is unknowable whether the prisoner suffers pain during administration of the drugs. As the U.S. Court of Appeals pointed out, there is always the risk of a cruel and prolonged death if, for example, there is "even a slight error in dosage or administration that can leave a prisoner conscious but paralyzed while dying, a sentient witness of his or her own asphyxiation." (Chaney v. Heckler, 718 F.2d 1174, 1983).

Most states use lethal injection as their sole or primary manner of execution. Nevertheless, a number of states still provide for execution by lethal gas; firing squad; electrocution; and/or hanging. In a few jurisdictions the prisoner is allowed to choose which method of execution he or she prefers. Ironically, most death certificates issued after a prisoner is executed lists homicide as their cause of death.

A table setting forth authorized execution methods categorized by state is set forth in the Appendix.

The number of states authorizing lethal injection increased from 17 in 1986 to 32 in 1996. Of the 358 prisoners executed from 1977 through 1996, the most common method of execution was lethal injection, which was used to execute 216 prisoners. In addition, 128 prisoners were executed by electrocution; 9 by lethal gas; 3 by hanging; and 2 by firing squad.

In 1996, 80% of all executions were by lethal injection, compared to 61% in 1986. Of the 70 executions carried out in 1997, 65 were by lethal injection, and the rest were by electrocution.

A table setting forth the number and method of executions conducted from 1977 through 1996 categorized by state, is set forth in the Appendix.

Viewing the Execution

Presently, thirteen states permit the family members of murder victims to watch the convicted prisoner's execution. Access is generally limited to the immediate family. In Oklahoma and Washington, family members are statutorily guaranteed the right to view the execution.

In the following states, however, an administrative hearing is held to determine access rights: California, Florida, Illinois, Louisiana, Montana, North Carolina, Ohio, Pennsylvania, Texas, Utah, and Virginia.

In addition, when authorized, Illinois allows families to watch only through closed circuit television.

The Abolitionist Movement

Although there has been a definite rise in death penalty sentencing in the United States since 1976, there has also been a strong countermovement towards its abolition by certain organized groups such as Amnesty International (AI) and the American Civil Liberties Union (ACLU). In addition,

Catholic, Jewish, and Protestant religious groups are among the more than 50 national organizations that constitute the National Coalition to Abolish the Death Penalty.

All abolitionist groups generally adhere to the ACLU position that the death penalty inherently violates the constitutional ban against cruel and unusual punishment and the guarantees of due process and equal protection under the law. They believe that states should not have the right to ceremonially kill in the name of justice, and that capital punishment is inconsistent with the fundamental values of our democratic system.

In addition, it is argued that despite efforts to rewrite the statutes, the application of the death penalty is necessarily arbitrary under our criminal justice system. In support of their position, they offer statistical evidence demonstrating that the death penalty is imposed disproportionately upon offenders who are poor, uneducated, or minorities.

In further support of abolition, it is argued that once a death sentence is carried out, it is clearly irrevocable if exculpatory evidence is subsequently uncovered. In that connection, abolitionist organizations attempt to prevent executions and abolish the death penalty through litigation, legislation and public awareness efforts.

A directory of organizations which support abolition of capital punishment is set forth in the Appendix.

CHAPTER 2:

THE FEDERAL DEATH PENALTY

In General

Between 1927 and 1963, the United States government executed 34 prisoners, including two women. However, there were no federal executions since the 1963 hanging of Victor Feguer in Iowa for kidnapping.

When the 1972 Supreme Court ruling in *Furman* declared the state death penalty statutes unconstitutional, the older federal death penalty statutes were similarly found to be arbitrary and capricious. The Federal government has since enacted a number of new statutes authorizing the death penalty.

1988 Drug Kingpin Statute

In 1988, a new federal death penalty statute was enacted for murders committed in the course of a "drug kingpin" conspiracy. This statute was carefully modeled after the Supreme Court approved state statutes enacted following *Furman*. Under the drug kingpin statute, six people have been sentenced to death, however, none have yet been executed.

1994 Crime Bill Expansion

In 1994, as part of an omnibus crime bill, the federal death penalty was expanded to include approximately 60 different offenses. Encompassed by the federal statutes authorizing a sentence of death are the following crimes: (i) murder of certain government officials; (ii) kidnapping resulting in death; (iii) murder for hire; (iv) fatal drive-by shootings; (v) sexual abuse crimes resulting in death; (vi) car jacking resulting in death; and (vii) running a large-scale drug enterprise.

According to the U.S. Justice Department, since the 1994 federal death penalty expansion, 243 cases have been reviewed for capital prosecution.

A table of federal death penalty offenses categorized by statute is set forth in the Appendix.

Race and the Federal Death Penalty

Since 1994, ten people have been sentenced to death under the expanded federal death penalty statutes. Seven of these ten defendants are Black, two are White, and one is Asian.

Of the sixteen men presently on federal death row, there are eleven Blacks, three Whites, one Hispanic, and one Asian.

According to statistics from the 1998 Federal Death Penalty Resource Counsel Project (FDPRCP), the first 119 federal death penalty prosecutions authorized by the Attorney General since 1988 have included 72 Blacks; 25 Whites, 17 Hispanics, and 5 Asians. This means that almost 80% of those prosecutions have been against minority defendants.

Disposition of the Cases

According to the FDPRCP, 46 of the federal death penalty cases were discontinued as capital cases after plea bargaining or other change in circumstances; 26 prisoners are on or awaiting trial; 23 prisoners received sentences less than death; 16 prisoners were sentenced to death and their executions are pending appeal; 9 prisoners were acquitted or the charges were dismissed; 2 prisoners died before sentencing; and 1 prisoner is awaiting resentencing after a reversal on appeal.

Method of Execution

Under the 1988 federal death penalty law, there was no particular method of execution set forth in the statute. In 1993, regulations were issued by President George Bush which authorized lethal injection as the method of execution under federal law.

However, the 1994 expanded death penalty law provides that the manner of execution will be the method employed by the state in which the federal sentence is handed down. If the particular state is a non-death penalty state, then the presiding judge is authorized to choose another state for carrying out the death sentence.

Appeals

As set forth in Chapter 11, there is only one appeal granted to a defendant as a matter of right—an appeal of the sentence and conviction to the U.S. Court of Appeals for the Circuit in which the case was tried. There is also only one chance to present any facts which may have been unavailable or neglected at trial.

All other review, such as U.S. Supreme Court review, is on a discretionary basis, and can only be requested once. An exception may exist in an extraordinary case where clear proof of innocence exists, or blatant constitutional violations occurred.

Native Americans

The use of the federal death penalty on Native American reservations has been left to the discretion of the tribal governments. Almost all the tribes have chosen not to use the federal death penalty. As of July 31, 1997, there were 46 Native Americans on state death rows.

U.S. Military

The U.S. military has its own death penalty statute, which employs lethal injection as the manner of execution. There are approximately eight men presently on military death row. Nevertheless, there have been no military executions conducted in over thirty years.

CHAPTER 3:

LEGAL REPRESENTATION

In General

It is often argued that the lack of adequate legal representation for indigent defendants facing the death penalty justifies abolition of capital punishment. It is a fact that approximately 90 percent of the prisoners facing execution on capital offenses cannot afford their own lawyer. Their fate is literally in the hands of an attorney who is assigned to represent the defendant for little or no compensation.

As set forth below, according to the Bureau of Justice Statistics' 1991 figures, the majority of prisoners—state, federal and local—are represented by some type of assigned counsel.

State Prisoners

Ninety-seven percent of state prisoners reported that they were represented by an attorney. Seventy-six percent of those who had legal counsel indicated that they were represented by a public defender or assigned counsel in connection with the offense for which they were now serving time. Among those represented by legal counsel, 79% of Blacks and 73% of Whites reported representation by an assigned attorney.

Federal Prisoners

Ninety-nine percent of federal prisoners reported that they were represented by an attorney. Forty-three percent of those prisoners were represented by private counsel, which accounted for nearly 50% of White prisoners and 33% of Black prisoners. The remaining federal prisoners—over 50%—were represented by a public defender or assigned counsel in connection with the offense for which they were now serving time.

Local Prisoners

Eighty-three percent of local jail inmates reported that they were represented by an attorney. Approximately seventy-five percent of those prisoners who had legal counsel indicated that they were represented by a public defender or assigned counsel in connection with the offense for which they were now serving time.

Some individuals may be fortunate enough to be assigned a lawyer who is relatively competent, and who has some experience in handling death penalty cases. However, more often than not, the attorney assigned to represent an indigent defendant facing the death penalty has little or no experience with capital offense cases, and may even be a recent law school graduate.

Although many assigned attorneys are dedicated to their client's case, there have been complaints that some assigned attorneys are so disinterested in these low or non-paying assigned cases, that they do not take the required time or make the necessary efforts to adequately represent the client.

Even worse, there are reported instances where attorneys assigned to death penalty cases have (i) failed to appear in court; (ii) appeared intoxicated in court; (iii) fallen asleep during the trial; and (iv) failed to make critical motions or obtain important exculpatory evidence that could have proved their client's innocence.

Nevertheless, even if the defense attorney has the necessary skills, and is dedicated to providing the client with the best representation, he or she is generally without the financial resources necessary to conduct an adequate investigation and defense. In addition, assigned defense attorneys usually handle a large caseload and cannot expend all of their energy on any one client's defense.

The widely broadcast "O.J. Simpson trial" demonstrated that the ability to retain expensive attorneys, experts and investigators can mean the difference between a conviction and an acquittal. Unfortunately, the indigent defendant can never realistically expect to receive this kind of defense. Providing the indigent defendant with an attorney who is fairly compensated, and further providing that attorney with the funds and resources necessary to conduct a thorough defense, is not a government or taxpayer priority. The result is that defendants who are unable to pay for the best defense are more likely to receive inadequate representation, and more likely to find themselves on death row facing execution.

Despite the Supreme Court's post-Furman approval of revised state capital punishment statutes, application of the death penalty based on financial resources results in an unfair and arbitrary outcome, which still disproportionately targets the poor, the less educated, and members of minority groups.

A table of characteristics of prisoners under sentence of death as of December 1996 is set forth in the Appendix.

The Adoption of Standards

In an effort to provide indigent defendants with a better chance at fair representation, particularly in death penalty cases, a number of states have adopted standards of qualifications for the representation of indigent defendants.

For example, Alabama requires that an attorney assigned to a capital case have no less than five years' prior experience in the active practice of criminal law. Nevada requires that the assigned attorney shall have had experience defending no less than seven felony trials, at least two of which involved violent crimes, including at least one murder case. Some states have standards which are minimal. For example, Idaho's statute merely requires that the attorney be licensed.

A table setting forth the states which have adopted standards of qualification in the legal representation of indigent defendants in capital cases, and details of their respective standards, is set forth in the Appendix.

Constitutional Guarantee

The sixth amendment establishes the right to legal counsel in federal criminal prosecutions. Through a series of cases, the Supreme Court has extended that right to state criminal prosecutions. A landmark decision was handed down in 1963 when the Supreme Court held that a defendant charged with a felony had the right to counsel (*Gideon v. Wainwright* 372 U.S. 335). In 1972, this right was extended to all criminal prosecutions—felony or misdemeanor—which carry a sentence of imprisonment (*Argersinger v. Hamlin*, 407 U.S. 25).

Indigent Defense Programs

Although the Supreme Court ruled that states must provide legal counsel for indigent defendants accused of a crime, there were no specific provisions on how to implement this task. The states have thus devised their own systems for providing counsel for poor defendants.

There are three primary systems used by State and local governments to provide legal representation to indigent defendants, including: (i) the public defender program—also known as "legal aid"—(ii) the assigned counsel program; and (iii) the contract attorney program.

Public Defender Program

Public defender programs are public or private nonprofit organizations which generally employ a full or part-time staff. Local public defenders often operate autonomously. Under a statewide system, an individual is usually appointed by the governor, and charged with developing and maintaining a system of representation for each county.

In 30 states, the public defender system is the primary method used to provide legal counsel to indigent criminal defendants.

Assigned Counsel Program

Assigned counsel programs involve the court appointment of private attorneys from a list, as the need arises. There are two types of assigned counsel programs: (i) Ad hoc; and (ii) Coordinated.

"Ad hoc" assigned counsel programs are those in which individual private attorneys are appointed by a judge to provide representation on a case-by-case basis. "Coordinated" assigned counsel programs utilize an administrator who oversees the appointment of counsel, and develops standards and guidelines for program administration.

Contract Attorney Program

Contract attorney programs involve agreements between governmental and bar associations, private law firms, and private attorneys, which provide legal services for indigent defendants over a specified period of time for a specific sum of money.

Federal Indigent Defense Program

As established by the Criminal Justice Act of 1964, the federal justice system provides indigent defense to eligible defendants through private attorneys, community defender organizations, and Federal Defender Services.

Bureau of Justice Statistics on Indigent Representation

Traditionally, assigned counsel systems and public defender programs have been the primary means to provide legal representation to the poor.

Among all prosecutorial districts, a public defender program was used exclusively in 28% of the cases, an assigned counsel system in 23% of the cases, and a contract attorney system in 8% of the cases. Forty-one percent of the prosecutors' offices reported that a combination of methods were used in their jurisdiction. The most prevalent was a combination of an assigned counsel system and a public defender program.

Costs of Indigent Defense

In 1979, state and local governments spent more than $350 million to provide legal services for indigent defendants, including expenditures for civil litigation. In 1990, state and local governments spent an estimated $1.3 billion for the same services.

CHAPTER 4:

PUBLIC OPINION

In General

According to surveys, American citizens overwhelmingly support the death penalty for serious crimes such as intentional murder. As a result, the death penalty has become an important political issue in national, state, local and even judicial elections. The majority of states, acting on what they believe to be the will of the people, have statutorily provided for capital punishment.

The federal government responded by expanding the federal death penalty and eliminating federal funding to death penalty resource centers, which were dedicated to defending death row prisoners, and instrumental in the release of a number of wrongly convicted prisoners on death row.

Rationale

Many reasons have been given for supporting the death penalty. The main arguments include (i) financial concerns—i.e., it is cheaper to execute a prisoner than to keep the prisoner in jail for the rest of his or her life; and (ii) deterrence—i.e. executions send a strong message to other potential criminals, discouraging similar behavior. Advocates of the death penalty also point out that executing the offender necessarily prevents him or her from committing further crimes. These factors are discussed further in Chapters 5 and 6 of this almanac.

Another primary reason the death penalty receives so much public support is the desire for revenge. The biblical adage—"An eye for an eye and a tooth for a tooth"—is often cited during discussions on capital punishment.

It is understandable that people who lose loved ones to murder cannot bear knowing that the murderer survives, however, this is not always the case. Murder Victims' Families for Reconciliation—a national organization based in Virginia—assists many individuals who have suffered the murder of a loved one, and who are seeking peace within themselves in an effort to replace the anger and hatred they feel towards the criminal.

Alternative Sentencing

Although there is significant public approval of capital punishment, polls have demonstrated that public support for the death penalty drops significantly when reasonable alternative sentences are offered.

According to a 1993 nationwide survey, 77% of the public approves of the death penalty. However, if offered an alternative sentence of life imprisonment without parole, with a minimum 25 years served, public support for the death penalty drops to approximately 56%.

If offered the alternative sentence of life imprisonment without any possibility of parole, public support drops further to 49% in favor of the death penalty. Moreover, if the public is offered an alternative sentence of life imprisonment without parole plus restitution to the victim's family, then support of the death penalty drops even further to 41%.

CHAPTER 5:

WEIGHING THE COSTS

In General

Death penalty advocates argue that executing a prisoner is far less expensive than paying for the offender's upkeep in prison for the rest of his or her life, and that abolishing capital punishment is thus unfair to the taxpayer. However, if one takes into account all the relevant costs associated with prosecuting a death penalty case to its conclusion, the opposite is true. Studies have demonstrated that capital punishment is a very expensive program to administer.

For example, a murder trial is usually much more protracted when death penalty is an issue. Further, a significant delay between the imposition of a death sentence and the actual execution is inevitable given the procedural safeguards required in capital cases. Post-conviction appeals in death-penalty cases are far more frequent than in any other cases.

The costs of litigation can also be tremendous, taking into consideration the time spent by judges, prosecutors, court reporters, defense counsel, jurors, and other court personnel. And, the instrumentalities needed to carry out an execution add further expense. The Federal Bureau of Prisons recently constructed one lethal injection chamber in Terre Haute, Indiana, at a cost of approximately $500,000.

Life Imprisonment: A Less Costly Alternative

As set forth below, a number of state and national studies have been conducted which support the argument that life imprisonment is a less costly alternative to capital punishment.

North Carolina - The most comprehensive study was undertaken by Duke University in 1993. The study concluded that pursuing a death penalty conviction costs North Carolina $2.16 million per execution more than the cost of a non-death penalty murder case with a sentence of life imprisonment.

There have been similar findings in other states where the death penalty has been vigorously sought:

California - According to a 1988 report by the Sacramento Bee, a California death penalty case adds an additional $90 million annually to the existing justice system costs, $78 million of which is incurred at the trial level.

According to a 1988 report in the Miami Herald, a Florida death penalty case costs an average of $3.2 million per execution.

Texas - According to a 1992 report in the Dallas Morning News, a Texas death penalty case costs an average of $2.3 million, which is approximately three times the cost of high security imprisonment in a single cell for 40 years.

Nationally, it is estimated that death penalty cases have cost taxpayers over $900 million dollars since capital punishment was reintroduced in 1976. Abolitionists argue that this money could have been better spent on programs designed to reduce crime. Even supporters of the death penalty denounce the additional costs of capital punishment.

However, the only way to make a death penalty case less expensive would be to limit the defendant's appellate rights. The result, however, would be to put many prisoners on death row who should not justifiably be executed.

As further set forth in Chapter 7, a number of innocent individuals would have been executed had they not been able to exercise their constitutionally guaranteed right to due process in order to demonstrate their innocence. In fact, almost half of the death penalty cases reviewed under federal habeas corpus provisions resulted in a reversal of the death sentence. Federal habeas corpus is discussed further in Chapter 11 of this almanac.

CHAPTER 6:

DETERRENCE

In General

A primary motivation underlying capital punishment is the logical notion that the threat of execution will prevent or discourage criminal behavior. However, although the death penalty necessarily guarantees that the condemned person will commit no further crimes, studies have shown that the death penalty has not had any appreciable deterrent effect on other criminals.

Causes

The explanations for this failed objective include the following:

1. A punishment can be an effective deterrent only if it is consistently and expeditiously undertaken. Capital punishment cannot be administered to meet these conditions unless a defendant is stripped of his or her constitutional rights.

2. The proportion of first-degree murderers under sentence of death is relatively small. An even smaller subset of this group have actually been executed. According to law enforcement authorities, death sentences imposed for murder only account for approximately one percent of all known homicides.

3. Most capital crimes are not premeditated — i.e, they are not planned. Thus, it is not plausible that the threat of punishment could deter a crime that usually occurs in the heat of the moment. In such cases, individuals often act without considering the consequences.

4. Terrorists often commit violent crime on behalf of strong religious, moral or political beliefs which tend to outweigh any concern for personal safety, and for which martyrdom is honorable.

5. Illegal drug traffickers are already involved in a dangerous and violent business in which the threat of death is a day-to-day reality whereas the remote threat of death as a criminal justice penalty is more illusive.

Incidence of Crime in Death Penalty States as Compared to Non-Death Penalty States

Studies have demonstrated that the death penalty is no more effective than incarceration in deterring murder, the primary offense for which most states impose a death sentence. In general, death penalty states as a whole do not have lower rates of criminal homicide than non-death penalty states. This is so even in adjacent states. For example, the homicide rates between 1990 and 1994 in Wisconsin and Iowa—non-death penalty states—were one-half the homicide rate of their neighboring state, Illinois, which is a death penalty state.

In addition, there is no statistical support for the notion that the death penalty deters murder of law enforcement officers. Between 1973 and 1984, lethal assaults against police officers were neither more or less frequent in death penalty states as compared to non-death penalty states.

Further, prisoners and corrections officers do not suffer a higher rate of criminal assault and homicide from life-term prisoners in non-death penalty states than they do in death-penalty states. Studies demonstrate that between 1992 and 1995, 176 prisoners were murdered by other prisoners, 84% of which were murdered in death penalty jurisdictions.

A 1995 nationwide survey of police chiefs revealed that they ranked the death penalty as the least effective means of crime control. Factors which ranked highest as a means to decrease the rate of violent crime included gun control, longer prison sentences, and the hiring of more police officers.

Suicide-by-Execution Syndrome

Abolitionists argue that in some instances the death penalty actually incites the capital crime it is supposed to deter. In support of this notion, they point to clinically documented cases of the so-called "suicide-by-execution syndrome." This syndrome involves individuals who would like to commit suicide but fear actually taking their own life. Thus, they commit murder for the sole purpose of having the death sentence imposed upon them.

CHAPTER 7:

INNOCENCE

In General

One of the primary arguments cited by opponents of capital punishment is the risk of executing an innocent person. The death penalty is the only sentence which cannot be remedied once carried out, if subsequent proof of innocence materializes.

Although some supporters of capital punishment believe that the death penalty is necessary even if an innocent person is occasionally executed, most argue that it is unlikely. However, a number of studies undertaken since the 1980's have demonstrated that innocent people are convicted of capital crimes, and that some have been executed before they could introduce evidence of their innocence.

In 1993, the Death Penalty Information Center (DPIC) prepared a report at the request of the House Subcommittee on Civil and Constitutional Rights regarding innocent persons on death row. The DPIC reported 48 defendants who had been released from death row in the prior 20 years because of subsequently discovered evidence of innocence. The report concluded that serious problems in the legal process led to such critical errors, and that there was a probability that these mistakes would continue to occur in the future.

The American Bar Association (ABA) has also conducted a number of studies concerning innocence and the administration of the death penalty. According to its research, numerous, critical flaws in current practices, coupled with the new federal habeas law and federal defunding of the death penalty resource centers, have compounded the problem of the conviction of innocent people. The ABA has concluded that executions must stop unless and until greater fairness and due process can be assured in death penalty administration.

Administration Problems

The following factors reportedly contribute to the risk that innocent individuals will be sentenced to death:

Expansion of Capital Crimes

There has been an expansion in the number of state and federal crimes leading to death sentences. In addition, more states have added the death penalty. More death sentences necessarily lead to more convictions of innocent defendants.

Lack of Defense Funding

There is a lack of funding for the defense of those accused of capital crimes. In order to put on an adequate defense, the attorney must have the resources to employ competent experts and investigators. This is often impossible when defending an indigent person. States have severely limited defense resources, and federal funding of the death penalty resources centers has been withdrawn.

In addition, defense lawyers must also be prepared at the outset to represent the defendant during the critical sentencing phase in the event that he or she is convicted. Thus, the attorney's time and efforts are split between getting an acquittal or preventing the client's death should he or she be convicted.

Narrowing of Appellate Rights in Capital Cases

Recent changes in the appeals process, particularly in federal courts, have made it more likely that executions will proceed despite evidence which points to a defendant's innocence. Both state and federal legislation threatens to severely shorten the length of time between conviction and execution of death row prisoners.

Currently, the average time between sentencing and execution is eight years. If that time is significantly shortened, executions will occur before there is any time to uncover evidence of innocence.

Politics

Politics play a big part in death penalty administration. Politicians and judges usually run on pro-death penalty platforms in an effort to garner public support.

In addition, prosecutors and police are under great pressure to solve the abhorrent crimes which generally constitute capital offenses, and the goal is to obtain a conviction.

Unreliable Evidence

There is usually a lack of eyewitness evidence to a capital crime, such as murder. Therefore, the prosecution must rely on less credible types of evidence to make its case. This includes testimony from generally unreliable witnesses such as accomplices to the crime, and fellow prisoners who may testify in return for some type of deal.

In addition, pressure by the police, or a defendant's mental illness or disability, can motivate an innocent suspect to offer false statements to satisfy the authorities. Therefore, a defendant's confession—often the primary evidence in a capital case—is not a dependable indicator of guilt.

Juror Bias

For a number of reasons, jurors may start out more inclined to convict the defendant in a capital case. Death penalty cases usually involve particularly brutal and shocking evidence which alone can outrage a jury and make it more likely that they will return a guilty verdict. Further, capital crimes which receive a lot of publicity may influence jurors by introducing them to inflammatory, inadmissible and incorrect information.

During voir dire, jurors are generally asked about their attitudes towards the death penalty. Jurors who are against imposing a death penalty will not be chosen to serve. The result is a jury who is ready and willing to return a death sentence. A recent study of jurors in death penalty cases found that the majority of jurors formed an opinion about the defendant's sentence before hearing any evidence at the punishment phase of the trial.

Statistics

As set forth below, the concern that innocent people will be sent to their death is supported by statistics which demonstrate that an increasing number of innocent defendants are being found on death row.

According to a 1987 study, 350 people convicted of capital crimes between 1900 and 1985 were innocent of the crimes charged. Some prisoners escaped execution by minutes, but 23 were actually executed during this period. Recent statistics reveal that the potential for unjustified executions is increasing.

Since 1973, approximately 6,000 people have been sentenced to death. Seventy-five people have been rescued from execution since 1970, after evidence of their innocence was uncovered. Twenty-one of those death row prisoners were released since 1993.

According to a 1996 report by the Department of Justice, many of the released prisoners owe their life to the diligence of their attorneys, who were able to use recently developed scientific technology—such as DNA evidence—to prove their client's innocence.

Unfortunately, most prisoners under sentence of death are not lucky or wealthy enough to receive the kind of dedicated legal representation necessary to put on an adequate defense. Expert testimony is costly, and not readily available to the indigent defendant.

Death Penalty Resource Centers

During the Reagan administration, death penalty resource centers were created to assist attorneys in vindicating the rights of innocent death row prisoners. The centers are dedicated to reinvestigating capital cases, and have successfully obtained the release of a number of condemned prisoners in many states. Until recently, there were twenty death penalty resource centers located across the country.

Unfortunately, federal funding for the resource centers has been withdrawn causing most of the centers to close their doors, although some of the centers try to continue with a reduction in staff, offering limited assistance.

Model Penal Code Recommendations

Following the 1972 *Furman* decision, when the U. S. Supreme Court overturned existing death penalty statutes, many states re-wrote their laws according to the recommendations set forth in the American Law Institute (ALI) Model Penal Code.

In the 1976 *Gregg* decision, when the Supreme Court began to approve of the newly rewritten death penalty statutes, the Court specifically referred to the Model Penal Code as a source for constructing a constitutionally acceptable statute.

The drafters of the Model Penal Code were aware of the danger that an innocent person could be convicted and sentenced to death by a jury despite the existence of "reasonable doubt." They addressed this concern by inserting a provision that permits the trial court to withhold a death sentence if there was evidence that left some doubt about the defendant's guilt, as follows:

Section 210.6 Sentence of Death for Murder; Further Proceedings to Determine Sentence.

(1) Death Sentence Excluded. When a defendant is found guilty of murder, the Court shall impose sentence for a felony of the first degree (i.e., a non-death sentence) if it is satisfied that: ... (f) although the evidence suffices to sustain the verdict, it does not foreclose all doubt respecting the defendant's guilt.

In its commentary, the ALI set forth its reasoning for inserting this provision:

> [S]usbsection (1)(f) . . . is an accommodation to the irrevocability of the capital sanction. Where doubt of guilt remains, the opportunity to reverse a conviction on the basis of new evidence must be preserved, and a sentence of death is obviously inconsistent with that goal.

Nevertheless, no state or federal jurisdiction adopted this provision, instead opting to include only a list of aggravating and mitigating circumstances for capital cases as also suggested by the Model Penal Code.

The Appellate Process

Once there has been a guilty verdict, the defendant loses the presumption of innocence. The appeal then focuses on the procedures that led to that guilty verdict. Federal courts reviewing a state capital case only review constitutional violations and do not consider new factual evidence pointing to innocence.

Most states require any new evidence of innocence to be produced within a set time limitation for consideration on appeal. For example, Virginia requires convicted defendants to produce new evidence within 21 days of the conviction.

Ideally, evidence of innocence should be uncovered before the defendant is convicted and sentenced to death. However, due to inadequate counsel and limited resources, this is often not the case. Unfortunately, if that evidence comes too late, it will often be rejected on technical procedural grounds, no matter how strongly it proves the defendant's innocence.

Case Studies

Rolando Cruz and Alejandro Hernandez

Rolando Cruz and Alejandro Hernandez were released in 1995, after spending more than 10 years on Illinois' death row. They had been arrested, prosecuted and convicted of the 1983 murder of a 10-year old girl in Chicago. Even though another man confessed to the crime shortly after their conviction, and despite the fact that their convictions and death sentences were repeatedly overturned on appeal, the prosecution continued to retry them. Three prosecutors and four police officers were subsequently indicted for obstruction of justice in the prosecution of their case.

Ricardo Aldape Guerra

Ricardo Aldape Guerra served 15 years on death row in Texas until a federal judge released him. The judge called Mr. Guerra's conviction "outrageous," and devised simply to achieve "another notch on the prosecutor's gun."

Wilbert Lee and Freddie Pitts

Wilbert Lee and Freddie Pitts were released from Florida's death row in 1975 following the confession by another man to the double murder for which they were convicted. They were subsequently released and received a full pardon from Governor Askew because of their innocence.

Randall Dale Adams

Randall Dale Adams was released from Texas' death row in 1989 after new evidence of his innocence came to light. The prosecutors declined to retry Adams.

Clarence Brandley

Clarence Brandley was released from Texas' death row in 1990. He was awarded a new trial when proof of racism, perjury and suppression of evidence during his trial was uncovered. After ten years on death row, all charges were dropped.

Gary Nelson

Gary Nelson was released from Georgia's death row in 1991. The county district attorney eventually acknowledged that there was no material element of the state's case in the original trial which had not been subsequently impeached or contradicted.

Kirk Bloodsworth

Kirk Bloodsworth was released from Maryland's death row in 1993. Bloodsworth was convicted and sentenced to death for the rape and murder of a young girl. He was first granted a new trial and given a life sentence. He was released after subsequent DNA testing confirmed his innocence. A year later he was awarded $300,000 for wrongful punishment.

Walter McMillan

Walter McMillan was released from Alabama's death row in 1993. The only evidence leading the police to arrest McMillan was testimony of an ex-convict seeking favor with the prosecution, although a dozen alibi witnesses had testified on McMillan's behalf. His conviction for murdering a white woman in 1988 was overturned on appeal after McMillan's attorney uncovered prosecutorial suppression of exculpatory evidence and perjury by prosecution witnesses, who subsequently retracted their testimony. The new district attorney joined the defense in seeking dismissal of the charges, concurring that the case had been mishandled.

Andrew Golden

Andrew Golden was released from Florida's death row in 1994. Golden's conviction was overturned when the Florida Supreme Court determined that the victim's death was nothing but an accident.

Jesse Tafero and Sonia Jacobs

In 1990, Jesse Tafero was executed in Florida following a 1976 conviction. He and his wife, Sonia Jacobs had been convicted of murdering a state trooper and sentenced to death. In 1981, Jacobs' death sentence was reduced on appeal to life imprisonment. In 1992, her conviction was vacated by a federal court. The evidence on which she and her husband had been convicted and sentenced consisted mainly of the perjured testimony of an ex-convict who turned state's witness in order to avoid his own death. Unfortunately, Tafero had already been executed by that time.

CHAPTER 8:

RACE

In General

In 1972, when the U.S. Supreme Court ruled in the *Furman* case that the death penalty was unconstitutional, it pointed out that racial discrimination was one of the grounds for its decision. Among other things, the Court held that the unlimited discretion allowed judges and juries in capital cases caused the death penalty to be applied in an "arbitrary and capricious" manner.

When the *Gregg* decision was handed down four years later, reinstating the death penalty, it held that the rewritten statutes provided adequate safeguards against arbitrariness and discrimination.

Nevertheless, subsequent evidence demonstrates that racial bias has continued to influence death sentencing. It is a fact that a disproportionate number of Blacks have faced execution on death row compared to their percentage of the total population. Between 1930 and 1996, 4,220 prisoners were executed in the United States; and more than half of those executed were Black.

Throughout the last century, Black defendants were routinely executed for offenses which would not have been considered a capital offense for a White defendant, such as rape. In fact, between 1930 and 1976, 455 men were executed for rape, and 405 of those executed were Black.

In addition, a greater number of Black juveniles were executed than White, and the rate of execution for Blacks who did not have any post-conviction appeal is also higher.

Although it is believed that this type of blatant racial bias no longer exists, present statistics demonstrate that Blacks still make up a disproportionately large percentage of death row prisoners. For example, of the 3,200 prisoners on death row in 1996, 40% were Black.

A table setting forth the number of prisoners under sentence of death categorized by race from 1968 through 1996 is set forth in the Appendix.

Statistics

From January 1977 through December 31, 1996, a total of 5,154 persons entered State and Federal prisons under sentences of death, among whom

51% were White, 41% were Black, 7% were Hispanic, and 1% were classified as "other."

During this same period, 358 executions took place in 27 States. Two-thirds of these executions occurred in only 6 States: Texas, Florida, Virginia, Missouri, Louisiana, and Georgia. Of that total, 200 were White, 134 were Black, 21 were Hispanic, 2 were Native American, and 1 was Asian. All executed prisoners were male except for one White female.

By the end of 1996, 34 States and the Federal prison system held 3,219 prisoners under sentence of death. Of that total, 1,820 were White; 1,349 were Black; 24 were Native American; 18 were Asian; and 8 were classified as "other." The 259 Hispanic inmates under sentence of death accounted for 8.8% of prisoners with a known ethnicity.

During 1996, 45 men were executed. Of those executed, there were 29 Whites, 14 Blacks, and 2 Hispanics. Thirty-six of the executions were carried out by lethal injection, 7 by electrocution, 1 by hanging, and 1 by firing squad. Virginia carried out eight of the executions; Missouri and South Carolina each executed six persons; Delaware and Texas executed three each; Arizona, California, Florida, Georgia, and Oklahoma executed two each; and Alabama, Arkansas, Illinois, Indiana, Louisiana, Nebraska, Nevada, Oregon, and Utah executed one each.

Prior Criminal History

The criminal history patterns of death row prisoners differed by race and Hispanic origin. Seventy percent of Blacks had a prior felony conviction as compared to sixty-four percent of Whites and fifty-seven percent of Hispanics. However, about the same percentage of all groups had a prior homicide conviction. Further, a slightly higher percentage of Hispanics and Blacks were on parole when arrested for their capital offense than Whites.

The Race of the Victim

Although Blacks continue to be sentenced to death and executed in far greater numbers than their proportion to the total population, many studies concerning this racial disparity suggest that the race of the victim is the decisive factor. Based on a number of studies, in 1990 the United States General Accounting Office concluded that prisoners on death row are more likely to have been convicted of a crime in which the victim was White.

According to a comprehensive study of racial discrimination and the death penalty in the state of Georgia, the odds of being sentenced to death were 4.3 times higher in cases were the victims were White. Thus, it is still a fact that the killing of a White person is treated much more severely than the killing of a Black person. This is so regardless of the race of the offender.

Since 1976, eighty-two percent of murder victims in cases where the convictions ultimately led to the offender's execution were White. This statistic is particularly troubling since less than half of all murders committed involve White victims.

The same does not hold true when the victim is Black and the offender is White. Since 1976, 84 Black defendants have been executed in cases where the murder victim was White, whereas only 5 White defendants have been executed in the same time period in cases where the murder victim was Black.

The most recent case involved the 1998 execution in South Carolina of John Arnold, a White man who raped and brutally murdered a Black hitchhiker, and carved the letters "KKK" into her body 20 years ago. An accomplice, John Plath, who is also White, is expected to be executed in mid to late 1998.

U.S. Supreme Court Justice Harry Blackmun, who was always a supporter of the death penalty even when it was outlawed in 1972, concluded that racial discrimination continues to corrupt the administration of capital punishment, stating: "Even under the most sophisticated death penalty statutes, race continues to play a major role in determining who shall live and who shall die."

CHAPTER 9:

WOMEN AND THE DEATH PENALTY

In General

Over the past twenty years, a very small percentage of women have been sentenced to death, and an even smaller number of women on death row have actually been executed. Statistics show that women are more likely to be dropped out of the system as they advance further through the phases of capital punishment case administration.

The rate of death sentencing of women is insignificant compared to men. Women receive the death sentence an average of 5 to 6 times per year, constituting only 2% of the annual total—e.g. since 1976, 113 women have been sentenced to death which is two percent of the total death sentences handed down during this period.

The rate of execution for women as compared to men is also insignificant. There have only been about 535 documented instances of female execution since 1632, which constitutes less than 3% of the total of 19,000 confirmed executions in the United States since 1608.

Statistics

Women account for about 1 in 8 murder arrests, which is 13% of the total. Nevertheless, women account for only 1 in 50 death sentences imposed at the trial level—i.e. two percent—and only 1 in 77 persons presently on death row, which is 1.3% of the total. Further, women account for only 1 in 437 persons actually executed since 1972, which is 0.5% of the total executions conducted during that period of time.

The 117 death sentences handed down against women between 1973 and 1997 have been imposed by 23 states. Two states—Florida and North Carolina—account for nearly one-fourth of all of these death sentences. Only 42 of the original 117 death sentences are currently in effect in 15 states. This constitutes only 1.5% of the 3,400 prisoners on death row, and less than 0.1% of women prisoners, which is estimated to be 50,000.

As set forth below, three of those sentences resulted in executions, and another 72 death sentences were reversed or commuted to life imprisonment.

The 42 women on death row range in age from 21 to 78, and have been on death row from between several months to over 15 years. Despite the rarity of female execution, a number of these women have nearly exhausted their appeals.

A table of the number of women prisoners under sentence of death as of December 1996 categorized by state and race is set forth in the Appendix.

Recent Cases

Only three women have been executed during the past 25 years. The most recently executed was Judy Buenoano, a 54-year old White women who was convicted of, among other things, poisoning her husbands with arsenic. Ms. Buenoano—known as the "Black Widow"—was executed in Florida by electrocution on March 30, 1998. She was the first women to be executed in Florida since 1838.

A month prior, on February 3, 1998, another White woman named Karla Faye Tucker was executed in Texas, after exhausting all of her appeals. Unlike Ms. Buenoano, there was a massive public movement to spare Ms. Tucker's life due to her apparently sincere conversion since her conviction for the brutal murder of two people with an axe. Nevertheless, her last minute petition for clemency was denied by Governor George Bush, and she was executed by lethal injection.

Prior to Ms. Tucker, the last woman to be executed in America was Velma Barfield. Ms. Barfield was executed by lethal injection in North Carolina in 1984 for murdering her fiancee.

These three women were the only females executed out of the 437 executions which have taken place since 1973. Prior to this, the last female offender executed was Elizabeth Ann Duncan, executed by California on August 8, 1962.

CHAPTER 10:

JUVENILE OFFENDERS

In General

Sixteen states permit the death penalty for offenders who are younger than 18 years of age. In 14 states, the death penalty may not be imposed unless the offender is 18 or older. The federal government also specifies age 18 as the minimum age for a death penalty sentence. Eight states do not specify any minimum age.

In 1988, the Supreme Court ruled that the impending execution of a juvenile in Oklahoma, who was 15 at the time he committed the crime, would be unconstitutional. However, in 1989, the Court upheld the death penalty for those who were 16 or 17 when they committed the crime.

Current Prisoners under Juvenile Death Sentences

As of December 31, 1997, 67 persons — all male — were under sentence of death in 12 different states in connection with their convictions for juvenile crimes. Their number constitutes approximately two percent of the total death row population of 3,400. All of the prisoners were convicted and sentenced to death for murder. The majority of victims were reportedly White adults, half of whom were female.

All of the condemned were either 16 or 17 at the time they committed the crime. Their ages now range between 18 and 39. Their time spent on death row ranges from several weeks to almost 20 years. Twenty-six of the juvenile offenders under sentence of death are in Texas, the largest number held in any one state's death row.

Although the total number of prisoners under sentence of death has increased almost 200% since 1983, the number of juvenile offenders on death row has not risen quite as rapidly. In 1983, there were 33 juvenile offenders under sentence of death compared to 67 today. This is attributed to the fact that the number of new juvenile death sentences each year is relatively equal to the number of death sentence reversals combined with executions.

A table of the number of prisoners under sentence of death as of December 1996 categorized by age at time of arrest is set forth in the Appendix.

International Use of the Death Penalty Against Juveniles

International human rights treaties prohibit anyone under 18 years old at the time of the crime from being sentenced to death. The International Covenant on Human Rights, the American Convention on Human Rights and the United Nations Convention on the Rights of the Child all have provisions to this effect. In addition, more than 100 countries either have laws excluding the execution of juvenile offenders, or are parties to one of these treaties.

Nevertheless, a small number of countries, including the United States, continue to execute juvenile offenders. In 1992, the United States ratified the International Covenant on Human Rights. However, with respect to Article 6 which prohibits the execution of persons whose crimes were committed when they were under eighteen years of age, the United States specifically reserved its right to impose capital punishment on such individuals.

According to Amnesty International (AI), only eight countries in the world are known to have carried out an execution of a juvenile offender since 1986, including: Bangladesh (February 1986); Iraq (December 1987); Nigeria (February 1989); Pakistan (November 1992); Saudi Arabia (September 1992); Yemen (July 1993); and the United States (December 1993). The majority of known executions of juvenile offenders—six since 1990—were carried out in the United States.

CHAPTER 11:

SENTENCE REVIEW

Automatic Review

Of the 38 states which have capital punishment statutes, 36 provide for automatic review of all death sentences regardless of the defendant's wishes. There are no automatic review provisions under the Federal death penalty procedures.

Arkansas and South Carolina do not undertake an automatic review of death sentences. In South Carolina, the defendant has the right to waive a sentence review if he or she is deemed competent by the Court.

While most of the 36 States authorize an automatic review of both the conviction and the sentence, Idaho, Indiana, Oklahoma, and Tennessee require review of the sentence only. In Idaho, review of the conviction has to be filed through appeal or forfeited. In Indiana and Kentucky a defendant can waive review of the conviction.

In Mississippi the question of whether a defendant can waive the right to automatic review has not been addressed, and in Wyoming neither statute nor case law clearly precludes a waiver.

If either the conviction or the sentence is vacated, the case is generally remanded to the trial court for additional proceedings or retrial. As a result of retrial or resentencing, the death sentence can still be reimposed at a later date.

Federal Habeas Corpus Review of State Court Criminal Convictions

A state prisoner can challenge the validity of his or her conviction and sentence by filing a habeas corpus petition in Federal court. Because this petition must have been first presented to the state court for review, the prisoner is relitigating previously resolved issues.

A habeas corpus petition generally alleges that the police, prosecutor, defense counsel, or trial court deprived the prisoner of a Federal constitutional right, e.g., the right to effective assistance of counsel; the right to a speedy trial, etc. Less than 1% of the sentences for which habeas corpus petitions are filed are death-penalty sentences. Most are custodial sentences, and more than 20% are life sentences.

The processing of a habeas corpus petition can take anywhere from one month to over 2 years before it is decided, depending on the number and complexity of the issues. A petition may be dismissed, however, if it fails to meet the procedural requirements of habeas corpus.

For example, prisoners must file a direct appeal in the state court for review before they are permitted to file a habeas corpus petition in the Federal court. This is known as the "exhaustion doctrine" because the prisoner is required to "exhaust" all state remedies before proceeding to the Federal level. This accounts for the majority of dismissals. However, there are other grounds on which a petition may be dismissed, including:

1. The failure to comply with court rules;

2. The failure to raise a cognizable issue;

3. The failure of the prisoner to be in custody;

4. The failure to raise issues that are within the court's jurisdiction; or

5. The issues presented in the petition are rendered moot.

Although a state's appellate court may have expended considerable time and resources in reviewing a conviction and/or sentence, lower Federal courts still have jurisdiction to review the state court criminal proceedings for possible violations of Federal constitutional provisions. Federal jurisdiction has been granted both by statute (28 U.S.C. 2241) and case law (Brown v. Allen, 344 U.S. 443 (1953)). However, according to the Bureau of Justice Statistics, very few petitions are granted. Thus, the validity of state court convictions remains relatively undisturbed.

If the petition is successful in Federal court, the Federal judge is empowered to issue a writ of habeas corpus directing certain relief, e.g., that the prisoner be released from custody, that the sentence be reduced, or that the case be remanded for retrial or resentencing.

For the past several years, the number of habeas corpus petitions filed in Federal district courts has equaled or slightly exceeded 10,000 cases—constituting 4% of the entire Federal district court civil caseload. Most prisoners filing the habeas corpus petitions have been convicted of violent crimes —e.g. homicide—and have been given a severe sentence. More than 20% of those prisoners had received a life sentence, including life with parole, life without parole, and life plus an additional number of years.

Prisoners with relatively short sentences—i.e. five years or less—are likely to be released before their habeas corpus proceedings have resolved.

The majority of habeas corpus petitions are brought by prisoners acting "pro se" — i.e., as their own attorney. A small percentage of prisoners are either represented by privately retained lawyers, assigned counsel, the ACLU, or some other anti-death penalty organization.

Although there is no constitutional right to an attorney in civil litigation, the court will generally request private attorneys to represent a prisoner when the legal issues are complex and an evidentiary hearing might be necessary.

Types of Issues Raised in Habeas Corpus Petitions

Based on a study of habeas corpus petitions brought in 1996, the Bureau of Justice Statistics has determined that the following issues are typically raised in habeas corpus petitions:

1. Ineffective assistance of counsel account for approximately 25% of all petitions.

2. Trial court errors account for approximately 15% of all petitions.

3. Fourteenth amendment issues account for approximately 14% of all petitions.

4. Fifth amendment issues account for approximately 12% of all petitions.

5. Sixth amendment issues account for approximately 7% of all petitions.

6. Eighth amendment issues account for approximately 7% of all petitions.

7. Prosecutorial misconduct accounts for approximately 6% of all petitions.

8. Fourth amendment issues account for approximately 5% of all petitions.

9. Miscellaneous other issues account for approximately 9% of all petitions.

Generally, the issues raised were primarily focused on the conduct of defense counsel and the state trial court judge, rather than on the prosecutor's behavior.

CHAPTER 12:

INTERNATIONAL VIEW

In General

While the U.S. has been expanding the number of death penalty eligible crimes, limiting appellate rights, and moving towards swifter executions, the international community has been moving away from the death penalty. As set forth below, the death penalty has been abolished, either by law or practice, in most countries outside the United States.

The Trend Towards Abolishing the Death Penalty

Since 1976, an average of two countries a year have abolished the death penalty, particularly for ordinary crimes. Capital punishment has been abolished, in law or in practice, in over one hundred countries worldwide.

The United Nations has called upon member states to abolish the death penalty, and the Vatican has condemned the widespread use of the death penalty. In addition, new countries joining the Council of Europe, including many former communist countries, must pledge to abolish the death penalty in three years.

According to Amnesty International (AI), 57 countries and territories have abolished the death penalty for all crimes; 15 countries have abolished the death penalty for all but exceptional crimes, e.g. wartime crimes; and 26 countries are abolitionist "de facto"—i.e., they retain the death penalty in law but have not carried out any executions for the past 10 years or more.

Although ninety-five other countries still retain and use the death penalty, the number of countries which actually execute prisoners in any one year is much smaller.

Countries Which Have Abolished the Death Penalty

Countries which have abolished the death penalty include: Andorra, Angola, Australia, Austria, Azerbaidzhan, Belgium, Cambodia, Cape Verde, Colombia, Costa Rica, Croatia, Czech Republic, Denmark, Dominican Republic, Ecuador, Finland, France, Georgia, Germany, Greece, Guinea-Bissau, Haiti, Honduras, Hungary, Iceland, Ireland, Italy, Kiribati, Liechtenstein, Luxembourg, Macedonia, Marshall Islands, Mauritius, Micronesia, Moldova, Monaco, Mozambique, Namibia, Netherlands, New Zealand, Nicaragua, Norway, Palau, Panama, Poland, Portugal, Principe, Romania, San Marino, Sao Tome, Slovakia, Slovenia, Solomon Islands,

Spain, Sweden, Switzerland, Tuvalu, Uruguay, Vanuatu, Venezuela, and the Vatican.

The following U.S. jurisdictions would also fall under this category: Alaska, District of Columbia, Hawaii, Iowa, Maine, Massachusetts, Michigan, Minnesota, North Dakota, Rhode Island, Vermont, West Virginia, and Wisconsin.

"Exceptional Crimes" Death Penalty Countries

The following countries have retained the death penalty, but apply it only for what are determined to be "exceptional crimes"—e.g., military crimes or crimes under emergency laws: Africa, Argentina, Brazil, Canada, Cyprus, El Salvador, Fiji, Israel, Malta, Mexico, Nepal, Paraguay, Peru, Seychelles, South Africa, and the United Kingdom.

"De Facto" Abolitionist Countries

The following countries are considered "abolitionist de facto," in that they retain the death penalty in law—i.e., "de jure"—but have not executed anyone for the past 10 years, or have declared a moratorium on executions: Albania, Central African Republic, Bermuda, Bhutan, Bolivia, Brunei, Congo Republic, Cote d'Ivoire, Djibouti, Gambia, Grenada, Madagascar, Maldives, Mali, Nauru, Niger, Papua New Guinea, Philippines, Rwanda, Senegal, Sri Lanka, Suriname, Togo, Tonga, Turkey, and Western Samoa.

The following U.S. jurisdictions would also fall under this category: Connecticut, Kansas, New Hampshire, New Jersey, New Mexico, New York, Ohio, South Dakota, Tennessee, the U.S. Federal Government, and the U.S. Military.

Countries Which Practice the Death Penalty

The following countries retain the death penalty both in law and in practice: Afghanistan, Algeria, Antigua, Armenia, Bahamas, Bahrain, Bangladesh, Barbados, Barbuda, Belarus, Belize, Benin, Bosnia-Herzegovina, Botswana, Bulgaria, Burkina Faso, Burundi, Cameroon, Chad, Chile, China, Comoros, Congo, Cuba, Democratic Republic, Dominica, Egypt, Equatorial Guinea, Eritrea, Estonia, Ethiopia, Gabon, Ghana, Grenadines, Guatemala, Guinea, Guyana, India, Indonesia, Iran, Iraq, Jamaica, Japan, Jordan, Kazakhstan, Kenya, Kuwait, Kyrgyzstan, Laos, Latvia, Lebanon, Lesotho, Liberia, Libya, Lithuania, Malawi, Mauretania, Malaysia, Mongolia, Morocco, Myanmar, Nigeria, North Korea, Oman, Qatar, Pakistan, Russia, Saudi Arabia, Sierra Leone, Singapore, Somalia, South Korea, St.

Christopher-Nevis, St. Lucia, St. Vincent, Sudan, Swaziland, Syria, Tadzhikistan, Taiwan, Tanzania, Thailand, Tobago, Trinidad, Tunisia, Turkmenistan, Uganda, United Arab Emirates, Ukraine, Uzbekistan, Vietnam, Yemen, Yugoslavia, Zambia, and Zimbabwe.

The following U.S. jurisdictions would also fall under this category: Alabama, Arizona, Arkansas, California, Colorado, Delaware, Florida, Georgia, Idaho, Illinois, Indiana, Kentucky, Louisiana, Maryland, Mississippi, Missouri, Montana, Nebraska, Nevada, North Carolina, Oklahoma, Oregon, Pennsylvania, South Carolina, Texas, Utah, Virginia, Washington, and Wyoming.

Reintroduction of the Death Penalty

Once abolished, the death penalty is rarely reinstated. Since 1985, only 4 abolitionist countries reintroduced the death penalty: Gambia, Nepal, New Guinea, and the Philippines. Nepal has since again abolished the death penalty. In the other three countries, there have been no executions since the death penalty was reinstated.

Death Sentences and Executions

According to Amnesty International, in 1996, 4,272 prisoners are known to have been executed in 39 countries, and 7,107 prisoners were under sentence of death in 76 countries. These figures are based only on cases known to AI, meaning the actual figures are likely much higher. For example, AI received unconfirmed reports of numerous executions in Turkmenistan and Iraq.

As usual, a small number of countries carried out the majority of these reported executions—3,500 in China; 167 in Ukraine; 140 in the Russian Federation; and 110 in Iran—accounting for 92% of all executions recorded by AI worldwide for 1996.

Effect of Abolition on Crime Rates

A 1988 study prepared for the United Nations concerning the use of the death penalty and crime rates concluded "that countries need not fear sudden and serious changes in the curve of crime if they reduce their reliance on the death penalty." In fact, recent crime figures from abolitionist countries fail to show that abolition has any harmful effects.

International Agreements to Abolish the Death Penalty

One of the most important developments in recent years has been the adoption of international treaties whereby countries commit to abolishing their death penalty. Three such treaties now exist, including: (i) The Sixth Protocol to the European Convention on Human Rights; (ii) The Second Optional Protocol to the International Covenant on Civil and Political Rights; and (iii) The Protocol to the American Convention on Human Rights to Abolish the Death Penalty.

The Sixth Protocol to the European Convention on Human Rights is an agreement to abolish the death penalty in peacetime to which 18 countries had signed on by mid-1995. The other two protocols provide for the total abolition of the death penalty but allow countries wishing to do so to retain the death penalty in wartime as an exception.

In its Second Optional Protocol to the International Covenant on Civil and Political Rights, the United Nations has declared that abolition of the death penalty will enhance human dignity and assist in the development of human rights.

APPENDICES

APPENDIX 1:

THE FLORIDA DEATH PENALTY STATUTE
FLORIDA STATUTES (1993)

SECTION 921.141 Sentence of death or life imprisonment for capital felonies; further proceedings to determine sentence.

(1) SEPARATE PROCEEDINGS ON ISSUE OF PENALTY.

Upon conviction or adjudication of guilt of a defendant of a capital felony, the court shall conduct a separate sentencing proceeding to determine whether the defendant should be sentenced to death or life imprisonment as authorized by s. 775.082. The proceeding shall be conducted by the trial judge before the trial jury as soon as practicable. If, through impossibility or inability, the trial jury is unable to reconvene for a hearing on the issue of penalty, having determined the guilt of the accused, the trial judge may summon a special juror or jurors as provided in chapter 913 to determine the issue of the imposition of the penalty. If the trial jury has been waived, or if the defendant pleaded guilty, the sentencing proceeding shall be conducted before a jury impaneled for that purpose, unless waived by the defendant. In the proceeding, evidence may be presented as to any matter that the court deems relevant to the nature of the crime and the character of the defendant and shall include matters relating to any of the aggravating or mitigating circumstances enumerated in subsections (5) and (6). Any such evidence which the court deems to have probative value may be received, regardless of its admissibility under the exclusionary rules of evidence, provided the defendant is accorded a fair opportunity to rebut any hearsay statements. However, this subsection shall not be construed to authorize the introduction of any evidence secured in violation of the Constitution of the United States or the Constitution of the State of Florida. The state and the defendant or his counsel shall be permitted to present argument for or against sentence of death.

(2) ADVISORY SENTENCE BY THE JURY.

After hearing all the evidence, the jury shall deliberate and render an advisory sentence to the court, based upon the following matters:

(a) Whether sufficient aggravating circumstances exist as enumerated in subsection (5);

(b) Whether sufficient mitigating circumstances exist which outweigh the aggravating circumstances found to exist; and

(c) Based on these considerations, whether the defendant should be sentenced to life imprisonment or death.

(3) FINDINGS IN SUPPORT OF SENTENCE OF DEATH.

Notwithstanding the recommendation of a majority of the jury, the court, after weighing the aggravating and mitigating circumstances, shall enter a sentence of life imprisonment or death, but if the court imposes a sentence of death, it shall set forth in writing its findings upon which the sentence of death is based as to the facts:

(a) That sufficient aggravating circumstances exist as enumerated in subsection (5), and

(b) That there are insufficient mitigating circumstances to outweigh the aggravating circumstances.

In each case in which the court imposes the death sentence, the determination of the court shall be supported by specific written findings of fact based upon the circumstances in subsections (5) and (6) and upon the records of the trial and the sentencing proceedings. If the court does not make the findings requiring the death sentence, the court shall impose sentence of life imprisonment in accordance with §775.082.

(4) REVIEW OF JUDGMENT AND SENTENCE.

The judgment of conviction and sentence of death shall be subject to automatic review by the Supreme Court of Florida within 60 days after certification by the sentencing court of the entire record, unless the time is extended for an additional period not to exceed 30 days by the Supreme Court for good cause shown. Such review by the Supreme Court shall have priority over all other cases and shall be heard in accordance with rules promulgated by the Supreme Court.

(5) AGGRAVATING CIRCUMSTANCES.

Aggravating circumstances shall be limited to the following:

(a) The capital felony was committed by a person under sentence of imprisonment or placed on community control.

(b) The defendant was previously convicted of another capital felony or of a felony involving the use or threat of violence to the person.

(c) The defendant knowingly created a great risk of death to many persons.

(d) The capital felony was committed while the defendant was engaged, or was an accomplice, in the commission of, or an attempt to commit, or flight after committing or attempting to commit, any robbery, sexual battery, arson, burglary, kidnapping, or aircraft piracy or the unlawful throwing, placing, or discharging of a destructive device or bomb.

(e) The capital felony was committed for the purpose of avoiding or preventing a lawful arrest or effecting an escape from custody.

(f) The capital felony was committed for pecuniary gain.

(g) The capital felony was committed to disrupt or hinder the lawful exercise of any governmental function or the enforcement of laws.

(h) The capital felony was especially heinous, atrocious, or cruel.

(i) The capital felony was a homicide and was committed in a cold, calculated, and premeditated manner without any pretense of moral or legal justification.

(j) The victim of the capital felony was a law enforcement officer engaged in the performance of his official duties.

(k) The victim of the capital felony was an elected or appointed public official engaged in the performance of his official duties if the motive for the capital felony was related, in whole or in part, to the victim's official capacity.

(6) MITIGATING CIRCUMSTANCES.

Mitigating circumstances shall be the following:

(a) The defendant has no significant history of prior criminal activity.

(b) The capital felony was committed while the defendant was under the influence of extreme mental or emotional disturbance.

(c) The victim was a participant in the defendant's conduct or consented to the act.

(d) The defendant was an accomplice in the capital felony committed by another person and his participation was relatively minor.

(e) The defendant acted under extreme duress or under the substantial domination of another person.

(f) The capacity of the defendant to appreciate the criminality of his conduct or to conform his conduct to the requirements of law was substantially impaired.

(g) The age of the defendant at the time of the crime.

(7) VICTIM IMPACT EVIDENCE.

Once the prosecution has provided evidence of the existence of one or more aggravating circumstances as described in subsection (5), the prosecution may introduce, and subsequently argue, victim impact evidence. Such evidence shall be designed to demonstrate the victim's uniqueness as an individual human being and the resultant loss to the community's members by the victim's death. Characterizations and opinions about the crime, the defendant, and the appropriate sentence shall not be permitted as a part of victim impact evidence.

(8) APPLICABILITY.

This section does not apply to a person convicted or adjudicated guilty of a capital drug trafficking felony under §893.135.

APPENDIX 2:

TABLE OF NON-DEATH PENALTY STATES

Alaska

Hawaii

Iowa

Maine

Massachusetts

Michigan

Minnesota

North Dakota

Rhode Island

Vermont

West Virginia

Wisconsin

District of Columbia

APPENDIX 3:

TABLE OF NUMBER OF PRISONERS EXECUTED IN 1996
CATEGORIZED BY STATE

JURISDICTION	NUMBER OF PRISONERS EXECUTED
Alabama	1
Arizona	2
Arkansas	1
California	2
Delaware	3
Florida	2
Georgia	2
Illinois	1
Indiana	1
Louisiana	1
Missouri	6
Nebraska	1
Nevada	1
Oklahoma	2
Oregon	1
Texas	3
South Carolina	6
Utah	1
Virginia	8
Total	45

Source: Bureau of Justice Statistics
http://www.ojp.usdoj.gov

APPENDIX 4:

TABLE OF NUMBER OF PRISONERS UNDER SENTENCE OF DEATH AS OF DECEMBER 1996 CATEGORIZED BYSTATE

JURISDICTION	NUMBER OF PRISONERS UNDER SENTENCE OF DEATH
Alabama	151
Arizona	121
California	454
Florida	373
Georgia	96
Illinois	161
Louisiana	63
Mississippi	57
Nevada	81
North Carolina	161
Ohio	170
Oklahoma	133
Oregon	18
Pennsylvania	203
South Carolina	68
Texas	438
Other jurisdictions	305
Total	3219

Source: Bureau of Justice Statistics
http://www.ojp.usdoj.gov

APPENDIX 5:

TABLE OF NUMBER OF PRISONERS UNDER
SENTENCE OF DEATH (1953 -1996)

YEAR	NUMBER OF PRISONERS UNDER SENTENCE OF DEATH
1953	131
1955	125
1956	146
1957	151
1958	147
1959	164
1960	210
1961	257
1962	267
1963	297
1964	315
1965	331
1966	406
1967	435
1968	517
1969	575
1970	631
1971	642
1972	334
1973	134
1974	244
1975	488
1976	420
1977	423
1978	483

YEAR	NUMBER OF PRISONERS UNDER SENTENCE OF DEATH
1979	595
1980	697
1981	863
1982	1073
1983	1216
1984	1421
1985	1589
1986	1800
1987	1964
1988	2111
1989	2232
1990	2346
1991	2466
1992	2575
1993	2716
1994	2890
1995	3064
1996	3219

Source: Bureau of Justice Statistics
http://www.ojp.usdoj.gov

APPENDIX 6:

TABLE OF NUMBER OF EXECUTIONS
CONDUCTED (1930 -1997)

YEAR	NUMBER
1930	155
1931	153
1932	140
1933	160
1934	168
1935	199
1936	195
1937	147
1938	190
1939	160
1940	124
1941	123
1942	147
1943	131
1944	120
1945	117
1946	131
1949	119
1950	82
1951	105
1952	83
1953	62
1954	81
1955	76
1956	65

YEAR	NUMBER
1957	65
1958	49
1959	49
1961	42
1962	47
1963	21
1964	15
1965	7
1966	1
1967	2
1968	0
1969	0
1970	0
1971	0
1972	0
1973	0
1974	0
1975	0
1976	0
1977	1
1978	0
1979	2
1980	0
1981	1
1982	2
1983	5
1984	21
1985	18
1986	18
1987	25

YEAR	NUMBER
1988	11
1989	16
1990	23
1991	14
1992	31
1993	37
1994	31
1995	56
1996	45
1997	74

Source: Bureau of Justice Statistics
http://www.ojp.usdoj.gov

APPENDIX 7:

TABLE OF CAPITAL OFFENSES
CATEGORIZED BY STATE

STATE	OFFENSE
Alabama	Intentional murder with 1 of 18 aggravating factors
Arizona	First-degree murder accompanied by at least 1 of 10 aggravating factors
Arkansas	Capital murder with a finding of at least 1 of 9 aggravating circumstances; treason
California	First-degree murder with special circumstances; train-wrecking; treason; perjury causing execution
Colorado	First-degree murder with at least 1 of 13 aggravating factors; treason; excluding persons determined to be mentally retarded
Connecticut	Capital felony with 9 categories of aggravated homicide
Delaware	First-degree murder with aggravating circumstances
Florida	First-degree murder; felony murder; capital drug-trafficking
Georgia	Murder; kidnaping with bodily injury or ransom when the victim dies; aircraft hijacking; treason
Idaho	First-degree murder; aggravated kidnaping
Illinois	First-degree murder with 1 of 15 aggravating circumstances
Indiana	Murder with 15 aggravating circumstances; excluding persons determined to be mentally retarded
Kansas	Capital murder with 7 aggravating circumstances; excluding persons determined to be mentally retarded
Kentucky	Murder with aggravating factors; kidnaping with aggravating factors
Louisiana	First-degree murder; aggravated rape of victim under age 12; treason
Maryland	First-degree murder, either premeditated or during the commission of a felony, provided that certain death eligibility requirements are satisfied

STATE	OFFENSE
Mississippi	Capital murder; capital rape; Aircraft piracy
Missouri	First-degree murder
Montana	Capital murder with 9 aggravating circumstances
Nebraska	First-degree murder with a finding of at least 1 statutorily-defined aggravating circumstance
Nevada	First-degree murder with 10 aggravating circumstances
New Hampshire	Capital murder
New Jersey	Purposeful or knowing murder by your own conduct; contract murder; solicitation by command or threat in furtherance of a narcotics conspiracy
New Mexico	First-degree murder
New York	First-degree murder with 1 of 10 aggravating factors; excluding persons determined to be mentally retarded
North Carolina	First-degree murder
Ohio	Aggravated murder with at least 1 of 8 aggravating circumstances
Oklahoma	First-degree murder in conjunction with a finding of at least 1 of 8 statutorily defined aggravating circumstances
Oregon	Aggravated murder
Pennsylvania	First-degree murder with 17 aggravating circumstances
South Carolina	Murder with 1 of 10 aggravating circumstances. Mental retardation is a mitigating factor
South Dakota	First-degree murder with 1 of 10 aggravating circumstances
Tennessee	First-degree murder
Texas	Criminal homicide with 1 of 8 aggravating circumstances
Utah	Aggravated murder; aggravated assault by a prisoner serving a life sentence if serious bodily injury is intentionally caused

STATE	OFFENSE
Virginia	First-degree murder with 1 of 9 aggravating circumstances
Washington	Aggravated first-degree murder
Wyoming	First-degree murder

Source: Bureau of Justice Statistics
http://www.ojp.usdoj.gov

APPENDIX 8:

TABLE OF FEDERAL DEATH PENALTY OFFENSES CATEGORIZED BY STATUTE

STATUTE	OFFENSE
8 U.S.C. 1342	Murder related to the smuggling of aliens
18 U.S.C. 32-34	Destruction of aircraft, motor vehicles, or related facilities resulting in death
18 U.S.C. 36	Murder committed during a drug-related drive-by shooting
18 U.S.C. 37	Murder committed at an airport serving international civil aviation
18 U.S.C. 115(b)(3)	Retaliatory murder of a member of the immediate family of law enforcement officials
18 U.S.C. 241, 242, 245, 247	Civil rights offenses resulting in death
18 U.S.C. 351	Murder of a member of Congress, an important executive official, or a Supreme Court Justice
18 U.S.C. 794	Espionage
18 U.S.C. 844(d), (f), (i)	Death resulting from offenses involving transportation of explosives, destruction of government property, or destruction of property related to foreign or interstate commerce
18 U.S.C. 924(i)	Murder committed by the use of a firearm during a crime of violence or a drug trafficking crime
18 U.S.C 930	Murder committed in a Federal Government facility
18 U.S.C. 1091	Genocide
18 U.S.C. 1111	First-degree murder
18 U.S.C. 1114	Murder of a Federal judge or law enforcement official
18 U.S.C. 1116	Murder of a foreign official
18 U.S.C. 1118	Murder by a Federal prisoner
18 U.S.C. 1119	Murder of a U.S. national in a foreign country
18 U.S.C. 1120	Murder by an escaped Federal prisoner already sentenced to life imprisonment

STATUTE	OFFENSE
18 U.S.C. 1121	Murder of a State or local law enforcement official or other person aiding in a Federal investigation; murder of a State correctional officer
18 U.S.C. 1201	Murder during a kidnaping
18 U.S.C. 1203	Murder during a hostage-taking
18 U.S.C. 1503	Murder of a court officer or juror
18 U.S.C. 1512	Murder with the intent of preventing testimony by a witness, victim, or informant
18 U.S.C. 1513	Retaliatory murder of a witness, victim or informant
18 U.S.C. 1716	Mailing of injurious articles with intent to kill or resulting in death.
18 U.S.C. 1751	Assassination or kidnaping resulting in the death of the President or Vice President
18 U.S.C. 1958	Murder for hire
18 U.S.C. 1959	Murder involved in a racketeering offense
18 U.S.C. 1992	Willful wrecking of a train resulting in death
18 U.S.C. 2113	Bank robbery related murder or kidnaping
18 U.S.C. 2119	Murder related to a carjacking
18 U.S.C. 2245	Murder related to rape or child molestation
18 U.S.C. 2251	Murder related to sexual exploitation of children
18 U.S.C. 2280	Murder committed during an offense against maritime navigation.
18 U.S.C. 2281	Murder committed during an offense against a maritime fixed platform
18 U.S.C. 2332	Terrorist murder of a U.S. national in another country
18 U.S.C. 2332a	Murder by the use of a weapon of mass destruction
18 U.S.C. 2340	Murder involving torture
18 U.S.C. 2381	Treason

STATUTE	OFFENSE
21 U.S.C. 848(e)	Murder related to a continuing criminal enterprise or related murder of a Federal, State, or local law enforcement officer
49 U.S.C. 1472-1473	Death resulting from aircraft hijacking

Source: Bureau of Justice Statistics
http://www.ojp.usdoj.gov

APPENDIX 9:

TABLE OF EXECUTION METHODS
CATEGORIZED BY STATE

STATE	METHODS OF EXECUTION
Alabama	Electrocution
Arizona	Gas Chamber, Lethal Injection
Arkansas	Electrocution, Lethal Injection
California	Gas Chamber, Lethal Injection
Colorado	Lethal Injection
Delaware	Lethal Injection
Florida	Electrocution
Georgia	Electrocution
Idaho	Firing Squad, Lethal Injection
Illinois	Lethal Injection
Indiana	Electrocution
Kansas	Lethal Injection
Kentucky	Electrocution
Louisiana	Lethal Injection
Maryland	Gas Chamber, Lethal Injection
Missouri	Lethal Injection
Montana	Hanging, Lethal Injection
Nebraska	Electrocution
Nevada	Lethal Injection
New Hampshire	Lethal Injection
New Jersey	Lethal Injection
New Mexico	Lethal Injection
New York	Lethal Injection
North Carolina	Gas Chamber, Lethal Injection

STATE	METHODS OF EXECUTION
Ohio	Electrocution, Lethal Injection
Oklahoma	Lethal Injection
Oregon	Lethal Injection
Pennsylvania	Lethal Injection
Rhode Island	Electrocution
South Carolina	Electrocution
South Dakota	Lethal Injection
Tennessee	Electrocution
Texas	Lethal Injection
Utah	Firing Squad, Lethal Injection
Virginia	Electrocution, Lethal Injection
Washington	Hanging, Lethal Injection
Wyoming	Lethal Injection

Source: Bureau of Justice Statistics
http://www.ojp.usdoj.gov

APPENDIX 10:

TABLE OF NUMBER AND METHOD OF EXECUTIONS CONDUCTED CATEGORIZED BY STATE (1977 - 1996)

STATE	NUMBER OF EXECUTIONS	LETHAL INJECTION	ELECTRO-CUTION	LETHAL GAS	FIRING SQUAD	HANGING
Alabama	13	0	13	0	0	0
Arizona	6	5	0	1	0	0
Arkansas	12	11	1	0	0	0
California	4	2	0	2	0	0
Delaware	8	7	0	0	0	1
Florida	38	0	38	0	0	0
Georgia	22	0	22	0	0	0
Idaho	1	1	0	0	0	0
Illinois	8	8	0	0	0	0
Indiana	4	1	3	0	0	0
Louisiana	23	3	20	0	0	0
Maryland	1	1	0	0	0	0
Mississippi	4	0	0	4	0	0
Missouri	23	23	0	0	0	0
Montana	1	1	0	0	0	0
Nebraska	2	0	2	0	0	0
Nevada	6	5	0	1	0	0
North Carolina	8	7	0	1	0	0
Oklahoma	8	8	0	0	0	0
Oregon	1	1	0	0	0	0
Pennsylvania	2	2	0	0	0	0
South Carolina	11	6	5	0	0	0
Texas	107	107	0	0	0	0

STATE	NUMBER OF EXECUTIONS	LETHAL INJECTION	ELECTRO-CUTION	LETHAL GAS	FIRING SQUAD	HANGING
Utah	5	3	0	0	2	0
Virginia	37	13	24	0	0	0
Washington	2	0	0	0	0	2
Wyoming	1	1	0	0	0	0
Total	358	216	128	9	2	3

Source: Bureau of Justice Statistics
http://www.ojp.usdoj.gov

APPENDIX 11:

DIRECTORY OF DEATH PENALTY ABOLITIONIST ORGANIZATIONS

NAME	CONTACT INFORMATION
Abolition Road	P.O. Box 10055
ACLU Capital Punishment Project	122 Maryland Ave. NE Washington
Amnesty International	322 Eighth Ave. New York, NY 10001 (Tel) 212-807-8400
Campaign to End the Death Penalty	P.O. Box 25730 Chicago, IL 60625
Catholics Against Capital Punishment	P.O.Box 3125 Arlington, VA 22203 (Tel) 703-522-5014
Death Penalty Education Center	12651 Briar Forest Suite 153 Houston,TX 77077 (Tel) 713-493-6232
Death Penalty Focus	74 New Montgomery Suite 250 San Francisco, CA 94105 (Tel) 415-243-0143/ (Fax)415-243-0994/ email: dpfocus@aol.com/ website: ttp://members.aol.com/ Dpfocus
Death Penalty Information Center	1606 - 20th St. NW, 2nd Fl. Washington, DC 20009 (Tel) 202-347-2531/ (Fax) 202-332-1915
The Endeavor Project	PO Box 23511 Houston, TX 77228-3511
Friends Committee to Abolish the Death Penalty	P.O. Box18106 Washington, DC 20036-1810
Human Rights Watch	1522 K St. NW Washington, DC (Tel) 202-371-6592

NAME	CONTACT INFORMATION
Illinois Coalition Against the Death Penalty	203 North LaSalle, #1405 Chicago, IL 60601 (Tel) 312-849-2279
Murder Victims' Families for Reconciliation	P.O. Box 208 Atlantic, VA 23303 (Tel) 804-824-0948
National Coalition Against the Death Penalty	918 F St. NW Washington, DC 20004 (Tel) 202-347-2411 (Fax) 202-347-2510
Oklahoma Coalition to Abolish the Death Penalty (OCADP -Oklahoma City Chapter)	PO Box 713 Oklahoma City, OK 73101
Oklahoma Coalition to Abolish the Death Penalty (OCADP -Tulsa Chapter)	3728 South Elm Place Suite 131 Broken Arrow, OK 74011
Oregon Coalition to Abolish the Death Penalty	PO Box 361 Portland, OR 97207-0361 (Tel) 503-232-8895
Texas Coalition to Abolish the Death Penalty	5018-B Antoine Suite #189 Houston, TX 77092 (Tel) 713-523-8454 Email: TCADP@adelante.com
The Washington Coalition to Abolish the Death Penalty (WCADP)	705 Second Ave., #300 Seattle, WA 98104

APPENDIX 12:

TABLE OF CHARACTERISTICS FOR
PRISONERS UNDER SENTENCE OF DEATH
AS OF DECEMBER 1996

CHARACTERISTIC	PERCENTAGE OF TOTAL
GENDER	
Male	98.5
Female	1.5
RACE/ETHNICITY	
White	56.5
Black	41.9
Hispanic	8.8
Non-Hispanic	91.2
Other	1.6
EDUCATION LEVEL	
8th grade or less	14.4
9th-11th grade	37.5
High school graduate	37.8
Any college	10.2
MARITAL STATUS	
Married	24.9
Divorced/Separated	21.3
Widowed	2.7
Never married	51.1

Source: Bureau of Justice Statistics
http://www.ojp.usdoj.gov

APPENDIX 13:

TABLE OF STATES WHICH HAVE ADOPTED STANDARDS OF QUALIFICATION FOR ATTORNEYS HANDLING CAPITAL CASES ON BEHALF OF INDIGENT DEFENDANTS

STATE	STATUTE	STANDARDS ADOPTED
Alabama	§13A-5-54 of the Code of Alabama	Any person indicted for a capital felony who is unable to afford a lawyer must be provided with a court appointed attorney who has no less than five years' prior experience in the active practice of criminal law.
Arizona	Rules of Criminal Procedure §6.5(c)	All criminal appointments must be made taking into account the skill likely to be required in handling a particular case. This rule is not limited to capital appointments.
Arkansas	§16-87-205 et seq	Attorneys must be on an approved list of the Capital, Conflicts and Appellate Office in order to handle capital cases and may not be excluded from the list solely as a result of inexperience.
California	§20 of the Judicial Administration Standards	Each Court of Appeals shall maintain three lists of qualified attorneys which specify the minimum qualification for the different types of cases. The rule further states that the Supreme Court shall maintain a list of attorneys for appointment in capital appeals. Attorneys appointed in capital appeals must have been in the active practice of law for four years in California state courts (or an equivalent experience); must have attended three approved appellate training programs including one program concerning the death penalty; must have completed seven appellate cases at least one of which was a homicide; and must have submitted two appellant's opening briefs written by the attorney, one of which involves a homicide, for review by the court or administrator.
Florida	§27.7001	The position of capital collateral representative has been created to represent indigent defendants in capital appeals. The capital collateral representative must have been, for the preceding five years, a member in good standing of the Florida Bar.

STATE	STATUTE	STANDARDS ADOPTED
Georgia	§17-12-39 of the Code of Georgia	No one may be assigned primary responsibility of representing an indigent unless licensed to practice in Georgia and is otherwise competent to counsel and defend a person accused of a crime. Uniform Superior Court Rule 29.8(E) states that cases in which the death penalty is sought shall be assigned only to attorneys of sufficient experience, skill and competence to ensure effective assistance of counsel.
Idaho	§19-856 of the Code of Idaho	Only attorneys licensed to practice in Idaho and are otherwise competent to defend a person may represent an indigent. This law does not specifically refer to capital cases.
Indiana	Criminal Rule 24	The presiding judge in a capital case must appoint two qualified attorneys to represent an indigent defendant. The lead counsel must be an experienced and active trial practitioner with at least five years of criminal litigation experience; have prior experience as lead or co-counsel in no fewer than five felony jury trials which were tried to completion; have prior experience as lead or co-counsel in at least one case in which the death penalty was sought; and have completed within two years prior to appointment at least twelve hours of training in the defense of capital cases in a course approved by the Indiana Public Defender Commission. Co-Counsel must be an experienced and active trial practitioner with a least three years of criminal litigation experience; have prior experience as lead or co-counsel in no fewer than three felony jury trials which were tried to completion; and have completed within two years prior to the appointment at least twelve hours of training the defense of capital cases in a course approved by the Indiana Public Defender Commission. In addition, appointed counsel for indigent defendants in capital cases must comply with an overall caseload limit.
Louisiana	Supreme Court Rule XXXI	In capital cases with an indigent defendant, the court must appoint no less than two attorneys to represent the defendant, both of whom must be certified by the Louisiana Indigent Defender Board as qualified in capital cases. One attorney shall be designated lead counsel and the other shall be designated associate counsel.

STATE	STATUTE	STANDARDS ADOPTED
Nevada	Nevada Court Rule 250 (IV)A	In a capital case, an attorney appointed to represent an indigent defendant must have skills adequate to represent the defendant with reasonable professional competence. The following are established as minimum requirements: The attorney shall have acted as counsel in no less than seven felony trials, at least two of which involved violent crimes, including one murder case; the attorney shall have previously acted as co-counsel in at least one death penalty trial; and the attorney shall have been licensed to practice law for at least three years.
New York	1995 Session Laws §35(b)	Two attorneys shall be appointed—one as lead counsel and one as associate counsel. The appointments shall be made from a list of four proposed teams of qualified lead and associate counsel provided to the court by the capital defender office.
North Carolina	N.C. Gen. Stat. 7A-459	No attorney shall be appointed to represent an indigent defendant in a capital case at the trial level unless he or she has a minimum of five years' experience in the general practice of law and who has not been found by the court or the public defender to be proficient in the field of criminal trial practice. No attorney shall be appointed to represent an indigent defendant in a capital case at the appellate level unless he or she has a minimum of five years' experience in the general practice of and who has not been found by the trial judge or public defender to have a demonstrated proficiency in the field of appellate practice.
Ohio	Common Pleas Court Rule 65	Trial counsel must consist of lead and co-counsel. Lead counsel must have extensive experience as lead counsel in felony cases, including experience in capital cases, as well as other requirements. Co-counsel must have extensive experience in felony jury trials. Two attorneys must also be appointed at the appellate level and must, among other requirements, have specialized training in defending capital cases.
Oklahoma	n/a	Standards of qualification are set by the Oklahoma Indigent Defense System Board.

STATE	STATUTE	STANDARDS ADOPTED
Oregon	n/a	Oregon has adopted standards patterned after the National Legal Aid and Defender Association's Standards for the Appointment and Performance of Counsel in Death Penalty Cases and the ABA's Guidelines for the Appointment and Performance of Counsel in Death Penalty Cases. Standard 3.1 (E) of Oregon's Qualification Standards for Court-Appointed Counsel to Represent Indigent Persons at State Expense lists the requirements for the appointing trial counsel in capital cases, and Standard 3.1 (I) lists requirements for counsel at the appellate level in capital cases.
Utah	Criminal Rule 8	Appointed counsel for an indigent defendant in a capital case must be proficient in capital cases. To demonstrate proficiency, at least one of the attorneys must have tried to verdict six felony cases within the past four years or twenty-five felony cases total, five of which must have been tried to verdict within the past five years. In addition, at least one of the attorneys must have appeared as counsel or co-counsel in a capital homicide case which was tried to a jury and which went to final verdict. Also, one of the appointed attorneys must have attended and completed within the past five years an approved continuing legal education course dealing with the trial of death penalty cases. Finally, the combined experience of the appointed attorneys must exceed five years in the active practice of law. In capital appeals for indigent defendants, at least one appointed attorney must have served as counsel in a least three felony appeals and at least one attorney must have attended and completed within the past five years an approved continuing legal education course dealing with the trial or appeal of death penalty cases.
Virginia	§19.2-163.8 of the Code of Virginia	All must be an active member in good standing of the Virginia State Bar, have extensive experience in litigation or appeals of criminal felonies and have had specialized training in capital litigation.

Source: http://www.ncsc.dni

APPENDIX 14:

TABLE OF PRISONERS UNDER SENTENCE OF DEATH
CATEGORIZED BY RACE (1968 - 1996)

YEAR	WHITE	BLACK	OTHER	TOTAL
1968	243	271	3	517
1969	263	310	2	575
1970	293	335	3	631
1971	306	332	4	642
1972	167	166	1	334
1973	64	68	2	134
1974	110	128	6	244
1975	218	262	8	488
1976	225	195	0	420
1977	229	192	2	423
1978	281	197	4	482
1979	354	236	3	593
1980	423	264	4	691
1981	498	354	8	860
1982	611	440	12	1063
1983	692	505	12	1209
1984	806	598	16	1420
1985	896	664	15	1575
1986	1013	762	25	1800
1987	1128	813	26	1967
1988	1235	848	34	2117
1989	1308	898	37	2243

YEAR	WHITE	BLACK	OTHER	TOTAL
1990	1368	940	38	2346
1991	1449	979	37	2465
1992	1511	1031	38	2580
1993	1577	1111	41	2729
1994	1653	1203	49	2905
1995	1730	1275	49	3054
1996	1820	1349	50	3219

Source: Bureau of Justice Statistics
http://www.ojp.usdoj.gov

APPENDIX 15:

TABLE OF NUMBER OF WOMEN PRISONERS UNDER SENTENCE OF DEATH AS OF DECEMBER 1996 CATEGORIZED BY STATE AND RACE

JURISDICTION	WHITE	BLACK	TOTAL
Alabama	3	1	4
Arizona	1	0	1
California	6	2	8
Florida	4	2	6
Idaho	1	0	1
Illinois	1	3	4
Mississippi	1	1	2
Missouri	2	0	2
Nevada	0	1	1
North Carolina	3	0	3
Oklahoma	3	1	4
Pennsylvania	1	3	4
Tennessee	2	0	2
Texas	4	2	6
Total	32	16	48

Source: Bureau of Justice Statistics
http://www.ojp.usdoj.gov

APPENDIX 16:

TABLE OF PRISONERS UNDER SENTENCE
OF DEATH AS OF DECEMBER 31, 1996
CATEGORIZED BY AGE AT TIME OF ARREST

AGE	NUMBER	PERCENTAGE
17 or younger	64	2.2
18-19	295	10.4
20-24	788	27.7
25-29	661	23.2
30-34	455	16.0
35-39	296	10.4
40-44	148	5.2
45-49	82	2.9
50-54	36	1.3
55-59	16	.6
60 or older	8	.3

Source: Bureau of Justice Statistics
http://www.ojp.usdoj.gov

APPENDIX 17:

DIRECTORY OF STATE
DEPARTMENTS OF CORRECTIONS

STATE	TELEPHONE NUMBER
Alabama Department of Corrections	334-240-9501
Alaska Department of Corrections	907-269-7400
Arizona Department of Corrections	602-542-5536
Arkansas Department of Correction	501-247-6200
California Department of Corrections	916-445-7688
Colorado Department of Corrections	719-579-9580
Connecticut Department of Correction	302-739-5601
District of Columbia Department of Corrections	202-673-7316
Florida Department of Corrections	904-488-5021
Georgia Department of Corrections	404-656-4593
Hawaii Department of Public Safety	808-587-1288
Idaho Department of Correction	208-334-2318
Illinois Department of Corrections	217-522-2666
Indiana Department of Correction	317-232-5715
Iowa Department of Corrections	913-296-3310
Kentucky Department of Corrections	502-564-4726
Louisiana Department of Public Safety and Corrections	504-342-6741
Maine Department of Corrections	207-287-4360
Maryland Department of Public Safety and Correctional Services	410-764-4003
Massachusetts Executive Office of Public Safety	617-727-7775
Michigan Department of Corrections	517-373-0720

STATE	TELEPHONE NUMBER
Minnesota Department of Correction	612-642-0200
Mississippi Department of Corrections	601-359-5621
Missouri Department of Corrections	406-444-3930
Nebraska Department of Correctional Services	402-471-2654
Nevada Department of Prisons	603-271-5600
New Jersey Department of Corrections	609-292-9860
New Mexico Corrections Departmen	505-827-8709
New York Department of Correctional Services	518-457-8126
North Carolina Department of Correction	919-733-4926
North Dakota Department of Corrections and Rehabilitation	701-328-6390
Ohio Department of Rehabilitation and Correction	614-752-1164
Oklahoma Department of Corrections	405-425-2500
Oregon Department of Corrections	503-945-0920
Pennsylvania Department of Corrections	717-975-4860
Rhode Island Department of Corrections	401-464-2611
South Carolina Department of Corrections	803-896-8555
South Dakota Department of Corrections	605-773-3478
Tennessee Department of Correction	615-741-2071
Texas Department of Criminal Justice	409-294-2101
Utah Department of Corrections	802-241-2442
Virginia Department of Corrections	804-674-3000
Washington Department of Corrections	360-753-1573

STATE	TELEPHONE NUMBER
West Virginia Department of Military Affairs and Public Safety	304-558-2037
Wisconsin Department of Corrections	608-266-4548
Wyoming Department of Corrections	307-777-7405

Source: http://www.bop.gov

APPENDIX 18:

DIRECTORY OF STATE GOVERNORS' OFFICES

STATE	GOVERNOR	ADDRESS	FAX	TELEPHONE	E-MAIL
Alabama	James Fob Jr.	State Capitol N-104, 600 Dexter Avenue, Montgomery, AL 36130-2751	(334)242-4541	(334)242-7100	govjames @afnmail.asc. edu
Alaska	Tony Knowles	State Capitol, P.O. Box 110001, Juneau, AK 99811	(907)465-3532	(907)465-3500	governor @gov.state.ak.us
Arizona	Fife Symington	State Capitol West Wing, 1700 W. Washington, 9th Fl., Phoenix, AZ 85007	(602)542-7601	(602)542-4331	azgov@gv. state.az.us
Arkansas	Jim Guy Tucker	250 State Capitol Bldg., Little Rock, AR 72201	(501)682-1382	(501)682-2345	mike.huckabee @state.ar.us
California	Pete Wilson	State Capitol, 1st Fl., Sacramento, CA 95814	(916)445-4633	(916)445-2841	n/a
Colorado	Roy Romer	136 State Capitol Bldg., Denver, CO 80203-1792	(303)866-2003	(303)866-2471	romer @goveror.state. CO.US
Connecticut	John Rowland	State Capitol, 210 Capitol Ave., Hartford, CT 06106	(203)524-7396	(203)566-4840	n/a
Delaware	Thomas R. Carper	Legislative Hall, Dover, DE 19901	(302)577-3118	(302)577-3210	n/a

STATE	GOVERNOR	ADDRESS	FAX	TELEPHONE	E-MAIL
District of Columbia	Mayor Marion Barry, Jr.	One Judiciary Square, 441 Fourth St. NW, Washington, D.C. 20001	(202)727-6561	(202)727-2980	n/a
Florida	Lawton Chiles	The Capitol, Tallahassee, FL 32399-0001	(904)488-9578	(904)488-4441	www.eog.state.fl.us
Georgia	Zell Miller	203 State Capitol, Atlanta, GA 30334	(404)656-2612	(404)656-1776	http:/www.state.ga.us/gov/
Hawaii	Benjamin J. Cayetano	5 State Capitol, Honolulu, HI 96813	(808)586-0006	(808)586-0034	n/a
Idaho	Phil Batt	State Capitol Bldg. West Wing, 2nd Fl., P.O. Box 83720, Boise, ID 83720-0034	(208)334-2175	(208)334-2100	governor@gov.state.id.us
Illinois	Jim Edgar	207 State Capitol Bldg., Springfield, IL 62706	(217)782-3560	(217)782-6830	governor@gov084r1.state.il.us
Indiana	Frank O'Bannon	206 State House, Indianapolis, IN 46204	(317)232-3443	(317)232-4567	FOBANNON@state.n.us
Iowa	Terry E. Branstad	State Capitol Bldg., Des Moines, IA 50319	(515)281-6611	(515)281-5211	n/a
Kansas	Bill Graves	Two State Capitol, Topeka, KS 66612-1590	(913)296-7973	(913)296-3232	Constituent@governor.wpo.state.ks.us
Kentucky	Paul E. Patton	100 State Capitol, Frankfort, KY 40601	(502)564-2517	(502)564-2611	n/a

STATE	GOVERNOR	ADDRESS	FAX	TELEPHONE	E-MAIL
Louisiana	Murphy J. Foster, Jr.	State Capitol, P.O. Box 94004, Baton Rouge, LA 70804-9004	(504)342-0002	(504)342-7015	lagov @linknet.net
Maine	Angus S. King, Jr.	State House Station 1, Augusta, ME 04333	(207)287-1034	(207)287-3531	governor @state.me.us
Maryland	Parris Glendening	State House, 100 State Circle, Annapolis, MD 21401	(410)974-3275	(410)974-3901	governor@gov. state.md.us
Massa-chusetts	William F. Weld	State House, Executive Office, Boston, MA 02133	(617)727-8685	(617)727-3600	wweld@state. ma.us
Michigan	John Engler	Olds Plaza, P.O. Box 30013, Lansing, MI 48909	(517)335-7899	(517)373-3400	migov@mail. state.mi.us
Minnesota	Arne H. Carlson	130 State Capitol, St. Paul, MN 55155	(612)296-2089	(612)296-3391	governor @state.mn.us
Mississippi	Kirk Fordice	P.O. Box 139, Jackson, MS 39205	(601)359-3741	(601)359-3100	n/a
Missouri	Mel Carnahan	216 State Capitol, P.O. Box 720, Jefferson City, MO 65102	(314)751-1495	(573)751-3222	constit@mail. state.mo.us
Montana	Marc Racicot	204 State Capitol, Helena, MT 59620	(406)444-4151	(406)444-3111	n/a
Nebraska	Ben Nelson	State Capitol, P.O. Box 94848, Lincoln, NE 68509-4848	(402)471-6031	(402)471-2244	n/a

STATE	GOVERNOR	ADDRESS	FAX	TELEPHONE	E-MAIL
Nevada	Bob Miller	Executive Chambers, Capitol Complex, Carson City, NV 89710	(702)687-4486	(702)687-5670	governor @govmail.state. nv.us
New Hampshire	Jeanne Shaheen	208-214 State House, Concord, NH 03301	(603)271-2130	(603)271-2121	n/a
New Jersey	Christine Todd Whitman	State House, Trenton, NJ 08625	(609)292-5212	(609)292-6000	www.tate.nj.us
New Mexico	Gary Johnson	State Capitol Bldg., Santa Fe, NM 87503	(505)827-3026	(505)827-3000	www. goveror.state. nm.us
New York	George E. Pataki	State Capitol, Albany, NY 12224	(518)474-3767	(518)474-8390	www.state. ny.us
North Carolina	James B. Hunt, Jr.	116 W. Jones St., Raleigh, NC 27603-8001	(919)733-2120	(919)733-4240	n/a
North Dakota	Edward T. Schafer	State Capitol, 600 E. Boulevard Ave., Bismarck, ND 58505-0001	(701)328-2205	(701)328-2200	ed_schafer @ndonline. com
Ohio	George V. Voinovich	Vern Riffe Ctr., 77 S. High St., 30th Fl., Columbus, OH 43215	(614)466-9354	(614)644-0813	n/a
Oklahoma	Frank Keating	212 State Capitol, Oklahoma City, OK 73105	(405)521-3353	(405)521-2342	governor @oklaosf.state. ok.us
Oregon	John Kitzhaber	254 State Capitol, Salem, OR 97310	(503)378-4863	(503)378-3111	n/a

STATE	GOVERNOR	ADDRESS	FAX	TELEPHONE	E-MAIL
Pennsylvania	Tom Ridge	225 Main Capitol Bldg., Harrisburg, PA 17120	(717)783-4429	(717)787-2500	governor @state.pa.us
Rhode Island	Lincoln Almond	State House, Providence, RI 02903	(401)273-5729	(401)277-2080	emaillincola @prodigy.com
South Carolina	David M. Beasley	State House, P.O. Box 11369, Columbia, SC 29211	(803)734-1843	(803)734-9818	governor @state.sc.us
South Dakota	William Janklow	State Capitol, 500 E. Capitol Ave., Pierre, SD 57501-5070	(605)773-5844	(605)773-3212	CathyS@gov. state.sd.us
Tennessee	Don Sundquist	State Capitol, Nashville, TN 37243-0001	(615)532-9711	(615)741-2001	dsundquist @mail.state. tn.us
Texas	George W. Bush	State Capitol, P.O. Box 12428, Austin, TX 78711	(512)463-1849	(512)463-1762	n/a
Utah	Michael O. Leavitt	210 State Capitol, Salt Lake City, UT 84114	(801)538-1528	(801)538-1734	gov_leavitt @state.ut.us/
Vermont	Howard Dean	Pavilion Office Bldg., 5th Fl., 109 State St., Montpelier, VT 05609	(802)828-3339	(802)828-3333	jbeagalio @state.vt.us
Virginia	George Allen	State Capitol, Richmond, VA 23219	(804)371-6351	(804)786-2211	governor @lmf.state.va. us
Washington	Gary Locke	Legislative Bldg., P.O. Box 40002, Olympia, WA 98504-0002	(360)753-4110	(360)753-6780	governor.locke @governor. wa.gov

STATE	GOVERNOR	ADDRESS	FAX	TELEPHONE	E-MAIL
West Virginia	Cecil Underwood	State Capitol Building, Charleston, WV 25305	(304)342-7025	(304)558-2000	n/a
Wisconsin	Tommy G. Thompson	State Capitol, P.O. Box 7863, Madison, WI 53707-7863	(608)267-8983	(608)266-1212	wisgov@mail.state.wi.us
Wyoming	Jim Geringer	State Capitol, Cheyenne, WY 82002-0010	(307)632-3909	(307)777-7434	governor@misc.state.wy.us

GLOSSARY

GLOSSARY

Abolish - To repeal or revoke, such as a law or custom.

Abstention - A policy adopted by the federal courts whereby the district court may decline to exercise its jurisdiction and defer to a state court the resolution of a federal constitutional question, pending the outcome in a state court proceeding.

Abuse of Discretion - A standard of review

Abuse of Process - The improper and malicious use of the criminal or civil process.

Accusation - An indictment, presentment, information or any other form in which a charge of a crime or offense can be made against an individual.

Accusatory Instrument - The initial pleading which forms the procedural basis for a criminal charge, such as an indictment.

Accuse - To directly and formally institute legal proceedings against a person, charging that he or she has committed an offense.

Acquit - A verdict of "not guilty" which determines that the person is absolved of the charge and prevents a retrial pursuant to the doctrine of double jeopardy.

Acquittal - One who is acquitted receives an acquittal,

Adjourn - To briefly postpone or delay a court proceeding.

Adjudication - The determination of a controversy and pronouncement of judgment.

Admissible Evidence - Evidence which may be received by a trial court to assist the trier of fact, either the judge or jury, in deciding a dispute.

Admission - In criminal law, the voluntary acknowledgment that certain facts are true.

American Bar Association (ABA) - A national organization of lawyers and law students.

American Civil Liberties Union (ACLU) - A nationwide organization dedicated to the enforcement and preservation of rights and civil liberties guaranteed by the federal and state constitutions.

Amnesty - A pardon that excuses one of a criminal offense.

Appeal - Resort to a higher court for the purpose of obtaining a review of a lower court decision.

Appellate Court - A court having jurisdiction to review the law as applied to a prior determination of the same case.

Arraign - In a criminal proceeding, to accuse one of committing a wrong.

Arraignment - The initial step in the criminal process when the defendant is formally charged with the wrongful conduct.

Arrest - To deprive a person of his liberty by legal authority.

Bill of Rights - The first eight amendments to the United

Capital Crime - A crime for which the death penalty may, but need not necessarily, be imposed.

Capital Offense - A criminal offense punishable by death.

Capital Punishment - The penalty of death.

Confession - In criminal law, an admission of guilt or other incriminating statement made by the accused.

Confrontation Clause - A Sixth Amendment right of the Constitution which permits the accused in a criminal prosecution to confront the witness against him.

Consent Search - A search which is carried out with the voluntary authorization of the subject of the search.

Conspiracy - A scheme by two or more persons to commit a criminal or unlawful act.

Conspirator - One of the parties involved in a conspiracy.

Constitution - The fundamental principles of law which frame a governmental system.

Constitutional Right - Refers to the individual liberties granted by the constitution of a state or the federal government.

Court - The branch of government responsible for the resolution of disputes arising under the laws of the government.

Criminal Court - The court designed to hear prosecutions under the criminal laws.

Cross-Examination - The questioning of a witness by someone other than the one who called the witness to the stand concerning matters about which the witness testified during direct examination.

Cruel and Unusual Punishment - Refers to punishment that is shocking to the ordinary person, inherently unfair, or excessive in comparison to the crime committed.

District Attorney - An officer of a governmental body with the duty to prosecute those accused of crimes.

Double Jeopardy - Fifth Amendment provision providing that an individual shall not be subject to prosecution for the same offense more than one time.

Due Process Rights - All rights which are of such fundamental importance as to require compliance with due process standards of fairness and justice.

Entrapment - In criminal law, refers to the use of trickery by the police to induce the defendant to commit a crime for which he or she has a predisposition to commit.

Exclusionary Rule - A constitutional rule of law providing that evidence procured by illegal police conduct, although otherwise admissible, will be excluded at trial.

Eyewitness - A person who can testify about a matter because of his or her own presence at the time of the event.

Fact Finder - In a judicial or administrative proceeding, the person, or group of persons, that has the responsibility of determining the acts relevant to decide a controversy.

Fact Finding - A process by which parties present their evidence and make their arguments to a neutral person, who issues a nonbinding report based on the findings, which usually contains a recommendation for settlement.

False Arrest - An unlawful arrest.

False Imprisonment - Detention of an individual without justification.

Federal Courts - The courts of the United States.

Felony - A crime of a graver or more serious nature than those designated as misdemeanors.

Felony Murder - A first degree murder charge which results when a homicide occurs during the course of certain specified felonies, such as arson and robbery.

Grand Jury - A group of people summoned to court to investigate a crime and hand down an indictment if sufficient evidence is presented to hold the accused for trial.

Habeas Corpus - Latin for "You have the body." Refers to a procedure brought by writ to determine the legality of an individual's custody.

Harmless Error - An error committed by a lower court proceeding which does not substantially violate an appellant's rights to an extent that the lower court proceeding should be modified or overturned.

Hearing - A proceeding during which evidence is taken for the purpose of determining the facts of a dispute and reaching a decision.

Homicide - The killing of a human being by another human being.

Hung Jury - A jury which cannot render a verdict because its members cannot reconcile their differences to a necessary standard, e.g. unanimity, substantial majority.

Illegal - Against the law.

Imprisonment - The confinement of an individual, usually as punishment for a crime.

Indictment - A formal written accusation of criminal charges submitted to a grand jury for investigation and indorsement.

Indigent - A person who is financially destitute.

Information - A written accusation of a crime submitted by the prosecutor to inform the accused and the court of the charges and the facts of the crime.

Informer - An individual who gives information concerning criminal activities to governmental authorities on a confidential basis.

Insufficient Evidence - The judicial decision that the evidence submitted to prove a case does not meet the degree necessary to go forward with the action.

Jail - Place of confinement where a person in custody of the government awaits trial or serves a sentence after conviction.

Jailhouse Lawyer - An inmate who gains knowledge of the law through self-study, and assists fellow inmates in preparation of appeals, although he or she is not licensed to practice law.

Judge - The individual who presides over a court, and whose function it is to determine controversies.

Jurisdiction - The power to hear and determine a case.

Jury Trial - A trial during which the evidence is presented to a jury so that they can determine the issues of fact, and render a verdict based upon the law as it applies to their findings of fact.

Legal Aid - A national organization established to provide legal services to those who are unable to afford private representation.

Lineup - A police procedure whereby a suspect is placed in line with other persons of similar description so that a witness to the crime may attempt an identification.

Malicious Prosecution - A cause of action against those who prosecuted unsuccessful civil or criminal actions with malicious intent.

Manslaughter - The unlawful taking of another's life without malice aforethought.

Minor - A person who has not yet reached the age of legal competence, which is designated as 18 in most states.

Miranda Rule - The law requiring a person receive certain warnings concerning the privilege against self-incrimination, prior to custodial interrogation, as set forth in the landmark case of "Miranda v. Arizona."

Misdemeanor - Criminal offenses which are less serious than felonies and carry lesser penalties.

Mistrial - A trial which is terminated prior to the return of a verdict, such as occurs when the jury is unable to reach a verdict.

Mitigating Circumstances - Circumstances that may reduce the penalty connected with the offense.

Modus Operandi - Latin for "the manner of operation." Refers to the characteristic method used by a criminal in carrying out his or her actions.

Nolo Contendere - Latin for "I do not wish to contend." Statement by a defendant who does not wish to contest a charge. Although tantamount to a plea of guilty for the offense charged, it cannot be used against the defendant in another forum.

Not Guilty - The plea of a defendant in a criminal action denying the offense with which he or she is charged.

Objection - The process by which it is asserted that a particular question, or piece of evidence, is improper, and it is requested that the court rule upon the objectionable matter.

Obstruction of Justice - An offense by which one hinders the process by which individuals seek justice in the court, such as by intimidating jury members.

Offense -Any misdemeanor or felony violation of the law for which a penalty is prescribed.

Pardon - To release from further punishment, either conditionally or unconditionally.

Parole - The conditional release from imprisonment whereby the convicted individual serves the remainder of his or her sentence outside of prison as long as he or she is in compliance with the terms and conditions of parole.

Penal Institution - A place of confinement for convicted criminals.

Perjury - A crime where a person under oath swears falsely in a matter material to the issue or point in question. @P = Plea Bargaining - The process of negotiating a disposition of a case to avoid a trial of the matter.

Polygraph - A lie detector test.

Premeditation - The deliberate contemplation of an act prior to committing it.

Presumption of Innocence - In criminal law, refers to the doctrine that an individual is considered innocent of a crime until he or she is proven guilty.

Prisoner - One who is confined to a prison or other penal institution for the purpose of awaiting trial for a crime, or serving a sentence after conviction of a crime.

Probable Cause - The standard which must be met in order for there to be a valid search and seizure or arrest. It includes the showing of facts and circumstances reasonably sufficient and credible to permit the police to obtain a warrant.

Prosecution - The process of pursuing a civil lawsuit or a criminal trial.

Prosecutor - The individual who prepares a criminal case against an individual accused of a crime.

Public Defender - A lawyer hired by the government to represent an indigent person accused of a crime.

Rape - The unlawful sexual intercourse with a female person without her consent.

Reasonable Doubt - The standard of certainty of guilt a juror must have in order to find a defendant guilty of the crime charged.

Restitution - The act of making an aggrieved party whole by compensating him or her for any loss or damage sustained.

Robbery - The felonious act of stealing from a person, by the use of force or the threat of force, so as to put the victim in fear.

Search and Seizure - The search by law enforcement officials of a person or place in order to seize evidence to be used in the investigation and prosecution of a crime.

Search Warrant - A judicial order authorizing and directing law enforcement officials to search a specified location for specific items or individuals.

Sentence - The punishment given a convicted criminal by the court.

Subornation of Perjury - The criminal offense of procuring another to make a false statement under oath.

Suppression of Evidence - The refusal to produce or permit evidence for use in litigation, such as when there has been an illegal search and seizure of the evidence.

Supreme Court - In most jurisdictions, the Supreme Court is the highest appellate court, including the federal court system.

Suspended Sentence - A sentence which is not executed contingent upon the defendant's observance of certain court-order terms and conditions.

Taking the Fifth - The term given to an individual's right not to incriminate oneself under the Fifth Amendment.

Testify - The offering of a statement in a judicial proceeding, under oath and subject to the penalty of perjury.

Testimony - The sworn statement make by a witness in a judicial proceeding.

Treaty - In international law, refers to an agreement made between two or more independent nations.

Trial - The judicial procedure whereby disputes are determined based on the presentation of issues of law and fact. Issues of fact are decided by the trier of fact, either the judge or jury, and issues of law are decided by the judge.

Trial Court - The court of original jurisdiction over a particular matter.

Unconstitutional - Refers to a statute which conflicts with the United States Constitution rendering it void.

Unreasonable Search and Seizure - A search and seizure which has not met the constitutional requirements under the Fourth and Fourteenth Amendment.

Vacate -To render something void, such as a judgment.

Verdict - The definitive answer given by the jury to the court concerning the matters of fact committed to the jury for their deliberation and determination.

Warrant - An official order directing that a certain act be undertaken, such as an arrest.

BIBLIOGRAPHY

BIBLIOGRAPHY AND ADDITIONAL READING

Black's Law Dictionary, Fifth Edition. St. Paul, MN: West Publishing Company, 1979.

Bohm, Robert M., *The Death Penalty in America: Current Research.* Cincinnati, OH: Anderson Publishing Co., 1991.

Costanzo, Mark, *Joint Revenge: Costs and Consequences of the Death Penalty.* New York, NY: St. Martins Press, 1997.

The Death Penalty Information Center (Date Visited: March 1998) http://www.essential.org/dpic/.

Haines, Herbert H., *Against Capital Punishment: The Anti-Death Penalty Movement in America, 1972-1994.* New York, NY: Oxford University Press, Inc., 1996.

Hood, Roger, *The Death Penalty.* New York, NY: Oxford University Press, Inc., 1996.

Latzer, Barry, *Death Penalty Cases: Leading U.S. Supreme Court Cases on Capital Punishment.* Woburn, MA: Butterworth-Heinemann, 1997.

The U.S. Department of Justice (Date Visited: March 1998) http://www.ojp.usdoj.gov/.